DIRT
FARMER
WISDOM

DIRT
FARMER
WISDOM

JOJO JENSEN

Red Wheel
Boston, MA / York Beach, ME

First published in 2002 by
Red Wheel/Weiser, LLC
368 Congress St.
Boston, MA 02210
www.redwheelweiser.com

Library of Congress Cataloging-in-Publication Data

Jensen, Jojo.
    Dirt farmer wisdom/Jojo Jensen.
        p. cm.
    ISBN 1-59003-015-X (alk. paper)
        1. Conduct of life. 2. Agriculture—Miscellanea. I. Title.

    BJ1581.2 .J46 2002
    170'.44—dc21   2001048468

Typeset in ITC Century Book

Printed in Canada

TCP

08 07 06 05 04 03 02
 7 6 5 4 3 2 1

The paper used in this publication meets the minimum requirements of the
American National Standard for Information Sciences—Permanence of Paper for
Printed Library Materials Z39.48-1992 (R1997).

TO MOM AND DAD WHO TAUGHT ME TO FOLLOW MY HEART,
CHASE MY DREAMS, FLY OVER ROADBLOCKS, AND PLAY IN THE DIRT.
I CAN'T SAY I LOVE YOU TOO OFTEN. I LOVE YOU.

ACKNOWLEDGMENTS

I couldn't have done it without each one of you. To my family, here and gone, biological and adopted. I love you and thanks. To all my pals who egged me on to keep going. To CP who taught me how to paint a picture and tell a story. To Gareth who hung in there for an entire year because she believed. To Jan, Robyn, and the Crew at Red Wheel/Weiser for every little detail. Thank you.

CONTENTS

Introduction to Farming

I n the 1930s, my grandparents had a subsistence farm in
Nebraska. They raised just enough food to feed their
family with little left over. Nothing was taken for
granted or wasted because there was nothing to throw
away.

They had no income. Their only source of cash came
from selling cream and eggs at the small town store in
Nystead. And that didn't happen often.

All they had was their land, home, and family. Yet they
were far from poor. They had pride, faith, a tangible sense
of self, with strong bonds to their family and community.

My grandpa, Bedstefar (pronounced *Bae-sta-fa*; it's
Danish for "grandfather"), was a simple "dirt farmer."
Carrying what he learned from his father and his father's
father, he passed on this rustic tradition and words of wisdom to my dad, Verl. Dad, in turn, cultivated his own
remarkable crop and instilled it in me.

Grandpa planted in dry land with no irrigation. He had
to carry water in or wait for rain. He sowed the land with his
hands and horses, not machinery. These toilsome duties
required resolve, tenacity, and endurance from every member of the family, six days a week, from sunrise to sunset. As
long as there was light shining on the barn, they worked.

Despite the farm's unending need to be tended, my family took Sundays off for church and socializing no matter what. Church was five miles away, and they went by buckboard. This was their day of rest.

Their basic, salt-of-the-earth philosophy carried them through the dark days of the Dust Bowl and the Great Depression, when they suffered the tragic loss of their farm, home, and neighbors.

Enduring financial ruin, they were forced to seek refuge and a new life in Oregon, where they knew no one, and the terrain was completely unfamiliar. But they took an abiding sense of humor along with what they could carry and the courage to forge ahead.

Grandpa suffered the ultimate loss. His young wife died in childbirth with their fourth son, who died as well.

Love and devotion to his surviving three sons gave him the drive to carry on. He carried an innate belief that life would get better.

Grandpa was right. Grandpa's relationship with his young sons grew into solid adult friendships. The boys graduated from high school with an ingrained foundation of work, responsibility, and joy.

When Dad was in college, he and grandpa double-dated and danced the night away. At the end of the night, Dad's dates would ask, "When are we going out with *your* Dad again?"

Grandpa died more than twenty years ago, but Dad keeps his father's "dirt farmer wisdom" very much alive.

When they married, Dad passed it on to my mom, Ann. They imparted those lessons to my brother and me.

Although our lives might appear more complicated and convoluted than the lifestyles of fifty years ago, dirt farmer wisdom takes us back to our roots and brings us down to earth, gently guiding us toward a simpler, more satisfying life.

Dirt farmer wisdom is as useful and true today as it was when it began. And it will be tomorrow. Lifestyles change, but genuine homespun common sense works every time. In a world full of alienation, noise, and cruelty, dirt farmer wisdom conveys a healthy dose of togetherness, reflective solitude, and kindness.

Farming is a reflection of the cycle of life. Farms burst with new life in spring, crops ripen during the long summer days, the harvest gathers overflowing bounty, and fields die back, sleeping until spring erupts again.

With the help of dirt farmer wisdom, you can experience the richness of cultivating your own life. Discover how to plan, plant, nurture, prune, and harvest what your life yields.

Love with Open Arms

CHAPTER 1

When the dirt farmer's daughter announces that she wants to go to college 1,000 miles away, he loves with open arms. He might grumble about out-of-state tuition, fuss over the impending phone bill and bemoan driving her all the way to school, but in the end he will open his arms and let her discover her own way.

A dirt farmer loves with arms open wide. He nourishes the strength, independence, and growth in those he loves. He encourages new ideas to germinate and nurtures personal exploration toward distant horizons, when in his heart all he really wants to do is hold on tight and never let go.

Loving with open arms is the foundation, the healing soil that sustains our crops. It provides nourishment for new opinions, solid ground in which to sink our roots, and a storehouse of understanding and humor for growth.

By loving people with open arms you encourage them to know who they are and what they want to achieve, and you empower them to love themselves and others fairly and gently.

〜⟁〜

*You can't save the horses from a burning barn
unless you stay alive and continue to protect yourself
as you rescue them from the flames.*

〜⟁〜

Before you can genuinely love others with open arms, you must nourish your own soul and value yourself. Grant yourself bottomless acceptance, endless understanding, infinite love and forgiveness so that when you do give of yourself, you offer love from a compassionate heart. When you tenderly cultivate love for yourself, you inherently pass on, by example, what is important to you.

I was an untamed tomboy growing up. Every pair of pants I pulled on sported holes and patches on the knees. When I fell on the cement and shredded my knees bloody, I ran to Mom.

She enfolded me in her waiting arms and assured me that I would be as good as new in no time. She cleaned my wounds, bandaged them for safekeeping, gave me another tight hug and peck on the head, then sent me outside to do battle once again with the sidewalk.

With her unbridled love Mom gave me the tools I needed to handle all the scrapes and bumps I would later find in the cruel world. Loving with open arms didn't mean that I was tied to her apron strings. It meant she instilled in me the courage to be self-reliant and to fight for who I am and what I believe.

Mom taught me how to walk out of a restaurant when the service was bad. How to fight for love when it's worth fighting for. And how to ask for help when my dreams were broken or my heart was bruised.

Loving with open arms also means being available to kiss life's little boo-boos without so much as an "I told you so." Knowing that you are loved is the armor you wear to face the world and you can extend that feeling to others.

You can love with open arms and still not accept self-destructive behaviors in yourself and other people. You can remain a safe haven for those people struggling, without allowing yourself to get sucked into the drama of their problems.

It's great to be a refuge from the stormy world, but be careful not to become someone's whipping post.

You can't take care of your own crops if you're spending all your time helping with your neighbor's neglected fields. No one eats if both harvests fail.

If your kid, parent, partner, or friend is an alcoholic or

drug addict, let them know that you will support them when they decide to take their life back. You aren't required to drive them to the rehab center to make sure they check themselves in, but when you love with open arms you might stop by with fresh-squeezed orange juice and a hug for support.

Loving with open arms can be risky. You can't fix anyone. You can't make anyone fit your picture of who you want them to be. You can't force the alcoholic to stop drinking, a junkie to stop shooting up, or a workaholic to stop slaving over a hot computer.

Those you love may never find their way back to you. All you can do is be there to welcome them with open arms when they are ready—ensuring them enduring shelter in your arms if they choose to return.

When you love with open arms, you stand firm in the healthy soil of love, with your roots sunk deep and your branches outstretched; you welcome and invite everyone to bask in your shade.

Open Hearts Cultivate Open Minds

CHAPTER 2

A dirt farmer has always planted a specific variety of dahlias in her garden. The blooms are abundant, the color spectacular. The dirt farmer knows she can look forward to beautiful flowers all summer long.

But, when she receives a catalog of plants, shrubs, and bulbs in the mail, and it shows the latest innovation in dahlias, she takes a look. The new bulbs take a bit more care with watering and fertilizer. But the flowers would be an amazing addition to her already kaleidoscopic garden.

Just because these new dahlias are a bit different, she doesn't dismiss the idea of adding them to her garden offhand. She opens her heart to the possibility of something new and colorful, then opens her mind to the information coming her way.

Open hearts cultivate open minds, when you know all flowers have a right to grow into their full bloom. Even weeds have their place in the garden.

My friends Dave and Lucy fell in love at summer camp. Lucy graduated from nursing school, and Dave taught second grade before heading into the wilds of summer camp. She was a sunny blonde with blue eyes, and Dave was a dashingly handsome African-American. They were a match made in campfire heaven.

When they married, his family embraced her as their new daughter. Her family disowned her.

His family couldn't wait to meet her and were already discussing future grandchildren. Her family didn't bother to meet Dave before they passed judgment.

Dave's folks threw a party in the garden of love. Lucy's parents barred themselves from entering the wedding celebration by closing their minds and hearts. The outcome of their bitter hearts was their vacant, silent home and their barren lives.

Welcoming hearts nudge open the gates
to the garden of understanding.

Our hearts unearth compassion, tolerance, and kinship. You can't hate your neighbors and treat them with malice and disdain, then expect them to come running to help when your chicken coop catches fire. You're only isolated because you choose to be.

You may feel that you don't fit in anywhere, so you don't even try. You might insist that only your beliefs are the right ones, while keeping other people and their opinions at arm's length. Or you could be simply too afraid to peek at what is growing on the other side of the fence.

You have the power anytime you choose to flip the latch, push the gate open, and discover what thrives on the other side, by entering the garden with an open heart and an open mind.

Assistance is everywhere if you want to open your heart and mind to tolerance, understanding, and love. A farm can't flourish without friends, neighbors, and allies. You can't scorn your mechanically gifted black neighbor, then expect him to come to your rescue when your tractor breaks down. You can't lie and cheat the people in your community and be surprised at the cold reception you receive at the chamber of commerce meeting.

With an open heart, you meet people on a level playing field. They will show you their true character, strong or weak, just as you will show them yours. Then you can decide how, or if, you want to deal with them.

Closed hearts and intolerance take a heavy toll on everyone in the community. The effects of hate and fear are far-reaching and all consuming. They pit neighbor against neighbor. Brother against sister. Friend against friend. They destroy.

We need one another to survive. We are interdependent, just as the plants, birds, and bees must be to keep the garden blooming. All things are possible with an open heart dwelling in the garden of love.

Just as the dirt farmer considers new flowers for her garden, you can overcome a barren, empty life by cultivating an open heart and mind.

When There's Room in Your Heart,
There Is Room in Your Home

CHAPTER 3

Dirt farmers never got rich. They raised only enough to take care of their families and put a little aside for the unexpected emergency. Feast or famine, they always maintained room in their hearts to help others when they could. Finding room in their homes was only a matter of shifting people around to make elbowroom at the kitchen table.

Finding room in your heart and home simply involves inviting people to join you. When your heart is inclined toward love, the screen doors naturally swing open.

Abandoned pets show up at the farm hungry, looking for a home. Heartless people dump unwanted animals in the country all the time. Kittens and dogs are left to fend for themselves in an unfamiliar and frightening world.

My family takes in strays—people and pets—until someone comes to claim them. Many never are claimed.

One evening, my dad was sitting in his comfy leather chair, when our first cat jumped through an open window, landing in Dad's lap. It scared the hell out of him. Bismarck immediately got comfortable, curled up, took a nap, and stayed forever.

Shadow, our second cat, showed up on the back porch, trying in vain to catch a bat in mid-flight for dinner. She was bone thin and hungry. Mom, who could never tolerate anything or anyone skinny, brought out some milk, some "I just happened to have this in the house" cat food, then found the cat a space to sleep in the barn. Today Shadow is part of the family, and skinny would certainly not describe her.

How do you deal with an abandoned creature? You can take it in, feed it, and hope the owner comes to his or her senses and comes looking for it. Or you can ignore it and hope it moves on.

It is easy to feel totally alone in our fast-paced, too busy to smell the roses world. Families are scattered all over the world like seeds to the wind, with schedules too tight for them to find their way home for the holidays. E-mail is great, but it isn't a home-cooked meal and a hug from Mom.

After college, I moved to Seattle to begin my career. I found a dusty basement apartment and, for the first time in my life, I was alone. Alone and scared. I barely left my little dark dwelling for the first three months. Work, grocery store, and home was my routine.

When Thanksgiving arrived, I was severely homesick. I wanted to go home so badly, I cried myself to sleep. I imagined the taste of Mom's turkey, her oyster stuffing and cranberries, but I had to work the day after Thanksgiving, so I couldn't leave. I was depressed. I thought I would spend the holiday all alone.

But my coworkers found room in their hearts and space at their Thanksgiving table for a geographical orphan and invited me over for an afternoon of turkey and football.

Sometimes a cow takes no interest in her calf. She decides not to feed it because it's just a bother. Someone has to feed that bleating baby five times a day if it is to mature into a healthy adult.

Sometimes that someone is you. Or me. Whoever has room in his or her heart and space in the barn.

Regardless of the time of year, our house welcomed my friends and my friends' friends. My brother Phil and I had rotating pals staying for dinner constantly. Even though my folks had limited resources, there was always enough to go around for one or two more hungry kids.

Dinner was full of loudly contested conversations about who was the best cartoon superhero or why girls are smarter than boys. One of us would come up with a snappy retort, and milk would inevitably erupt from someone's nose and the impossible-to-stop laughing fits would begin.

On rainy, cold, winter Saturdays Mom and Dad packed the ever-ready picnic basket and a flock of kids into the wood-sided station wagon and headed out to a familiar park on the Columbia Gorge. We jumped out of the car, scouted the area, threw rocks in the water, and ate bologna sandwiches all afternoon. Mom and Dad sat and talked under an old log shelter, while we ran around chasing each other like maniacs. Dad used to call it "blowing a little stink off." Later in the afternoon, we piled back in the car for a quiet ride home. When it came time for these family rookies[*] to move on, Mom and Dad dished out hugs, kisses, and wishes for success. No tears, no regrets. These kids, now adults, have become permanent leaves on the branches of our family tree.

You can provide a safe haven when people need help or support. Help can be a glowing letter of recommendation for a college applicant, or a care package to a friend who is far away from home. Support can be a place to live for a close friend wrestling with divorce, or it can be moral support to help someone stay away from drugs and alcohol.

Finding room in your heart also means finding space in your schedule for yourself.

*You can't feed your friends
if your own crops aren't growing.*

---

[*] Family rookies are people who have no idea what a "healthy family" is. Rookies discover what is important to them by being around people who support them, challenge them, and help them find their road.

Take yourself to a movie. Buy yourself a cup of coffee and watch other people scurrying about. Indulge in a bubble bath. Take pleasure refilling your reserve tanks of love and recharging your batteries of understanding.

It's the little gestures that have tremendous impact when you find space in your heart for others. Make time for a quick latté with a friend who is feeling low. Surprise her! Deliver it personally. Find room at the dinner table for people who don't have anywhere to go for Passover Seder. Give your friend a ride to pick up her car after work. Invite the new single mom on the block over for a play date.

≡≡≡≡≡≡➤

When there is room in your heart,
the room in your home expands endlessly.

Can't Have Rainbows Without Rain

CHAPTER 4

Few crops make it to the marketplace without unexpected hitches or a few broken stalks. You can't let flat tires on your tractor or rough roads stop you when you have to get your harvest to market.

Confronting personal and professional storms tests your resolve to keep marching toward your goals. You have the power to decide if you want to stop, push forward, or choose a different direction.

When you finally break through the thick black clouds of blinding rain or hailstones, you discover the clear blue sky with the crisp prism of a rainbow waiting for you.

Your survival is a daily reminder of your drive, visions, and achievement.

When you see a rainbow, you see the dazzling spectrum of light and colors. You don't think about the pounding rain that it took to create that brilliant arc that lies above the pot of gold.

My brother Phil is one of my constant role models. He lives in the rainbow, quietly protecting his family against any approaching storms.

Phil survived his arduous college years at the University

of Oregon and was rewarded with a hard-earned bachelor's degree in biochemistry. Then he headed east to St. Louis, Missouri, to attend dental school. He focused his concentration on his classes and had little time for other pursuits. Yet he still found time to explore and enjoy his new surroundings, forging many lifelong friendships in the process. Despite his tight schedule and his diligent study habits, he fell in love.

Phil and Beth got married one week after his graduation. That would have been enough for most people, but not my brother. He hadn't reached his ultimate goal yet.

The newlyweds moved to Chicago for his internship in oral surgery. That meant uprooting Beth from her hometown and finding himself again in an unfamiliar city, knowing no one.

Phil's hours were grueling. The neighborhood in which he and Beth lived may have been frightening, with constant car alarms blaring, intermittent gunfire and gang activity, but the training he received was unbeatable.

He worked through sporadic squalls of doubt and frustration to follow his dreams of becoming an oral surgeon to the end. The long hours working in the ER took a toll on his marriage. He questioned whether he should stop his training as an oral surgeon, and become a general dentist and focus on his family.

He didn't finish with his training until he was in his thirties. Most people are established in their careers and families at that point. He had to start at the bottom of the professional ladder with his first oral surgery position in Portland, Oregon.

His rainbow colors blazing, Phil conquered all the storms that came his way. Today he operates his own flourishing oral surgery practice in Mattoon, Illinois. Phil weathered the challenges of starting a new business and family while passing safely though periodic thunderclouds, relishing life in the dazzling spectrum.

Everyone encounters storms. To survive them you must have the courage and commitment to ride them out.

*If a tornado rips your barn from the foundation,
you can give up or rebuild. If you give up,
you have to move. If you rebuild, you can throw one hell
of a party and get a new barn in the process.*

If you get laid off after thirty years of devoted service, you can take your severance check and give up, or you can pursue the dream job you've always wanted but never took the time to explore.

If you are an artist of any kind—writer, actor, painter, cartoonist—you will encounter at least one person who will tell you that you have no talent and you should quit. Protect your work, your art, and yourself as you would a vulnerable child. Run away from people who ridicule, discourage, sabotage, or disparage you or your work. (Check out *The Artist's Way* by Julie Cameron . . . a must read). Follow your heart with bold persistence through the gusts of naysayers and prophets of gloom.

There is no such thing as an overnight sensation. Trust me, anyone who has achieved recognition in his or her field has toiled long and hard to get there.

It takes time and the right mixture of fertilizers to get the pH of the soil just right for plants to flourish and flowers to bloom.

Don't allow storms of fear, disbelief, or other people's opinions stop you in your quest. These temporary tempests dissipate with the winds of desire, and purpose blows those black clouds out of your path.

Meet the storms head-on, push through the rain and wind to dance in the glorious colors of the rainbow.

Make Hay While the Sun's Shining

CHAPTER 5

Cutting hay is tricky on the Oregon coast. You have to have good weather for at least ten days or the hay rots in the field before you get a chance to bail it.

If you don't make hay when the sun is shining,
you pay a high price come winter.

On a farm, chores need to be done every day, with no exception. Animals need feeding, fields need tending, and fences need mending. On the farm, today is what matters. Yesterday is gone and tomorrow will take care of itself if you do the work today.

What are you doing today? Are you wasting your precious time with people you don't really like or who don't genuinely like you? Or are you spending it with people you love and who love you back? Are you fuming over what you can't change? Or are you working daily at what you can? Is your mind lost in what may happen tomorrow? Or are you focused on what you can do to make your life happier today?

Today is it! Make the most of the moments you have. Yesterday only has control over you if you allow it to influence you today.

Planning for tomorrow, envisioning your dreams and goals is important. But worrying about tomorrow, something you have no control over, can only interfere with your living to your fullest potential today.

Living for today isn't easy. We spend so much time running around picking up dry cleaning, doing dishes, or surfing the net, that we forget to sit down, turn off the TV, and talk with our family or spend a little quality time by ourselves. Today silently slips away if we don't pay attention.

Grandma died when Dad was ten. Her death came as a shock to everyone, but it hit Dad especially hard because he was so young. He could have spent a lifetime mourning his mother and grieving the closeness he would never know. But Grandpa wouldn't let that happen.

He knew that life moved on. He chose to create a life of joy and laughter for him and his boys, not to live in sorrow. Grandpa helped his sons grieve for their lost mother, but with his strength and persistence, they all moved on, never forgetting the woman they all loved so deeply.

Don't wait for tragedy to strike. Live for today. Women who beat breast cancer or couples who face the loss of a child realize how precious the small moments are.

Time is not for wasting. Make joy while the sun shines.

Taking time to watch a sunset, daydream, meditate, or spend a quiet moment by yourself is never a waste of time when you do it mindfully. Be conscious of each moment of your life.

Focusing too much on the past or future will rob you of amazing people, marvelous adventures, and the gut-wrenching challenges in your life right now.

I already have my acceptance speech written for the best original screenplay Oscar™ I plan to win. But that speech won't do me any good if I don't sit down and write my award-winning movie today.

Begin your life today. Enjoy each and every moment you share with the people you love right now. Don't wait for a more convenient time or location. Make sure they know how you feel.

Acknowledge your past for what it was. Plan your future for what you want it to be. Remember to embrace today. Make hay when the sun shines, then relax when the barn is brimming with bales.

Don't Let Virtues Overshadow Vision

CHAPTER 6

*Vision is what convinces you to grow wheat
when everyone else in the valley is planting corn.*

V isions are what you see in your mind's eye—what you believe a situation should look like or what an outcome should be for you.

Your vision can be an educated one, such as realizing the nutrients in the soil will be replenished by rotating your crops and planting wheat. It can be a spiritual or an imagined vision, where you have no exact or material reason upon which to base it.

Virtues can help you realize your visions when they are applied in balance like fertilizer. When used skillfully, fertilizer enriches the soil. But using too much can scorch the ground.

Virtues are active qualities. They create the framework of who you are, how you see the world, and how you ultimately deal with it. Not actively expressing your virtues results in a hollow and lonely life:

- Fertilizer that never hits the ground doesn't help anything grow.
- Compassion unexpressed is indifference.
- Perseverance not set in motion is worthless.
- Courage not acted upon is useless.
- Responsibility unexercised is pointless.
- Respect not applied is neglect.

Virtues build the foundation that forms your character. Watering your crop is crucial to its survival. If you overwater or underwater it, however, the result is the same as if you did not water it at all. Virtues taken to extremes will overshadow a vision, no matter how positive the concept.

- *Love* taken to extremes becomes hate. It overshadows the tender vision of a supportive, caring, loving relationship. This extreme shows up as jealousy, control, possessiveness, and domestic violence. Ultimately it destroys everything it claims to love.
- A *work ethic* taken to extremes becomes an addiction. It overshadows the balanced vision of a fulfilling, exciting, and profitable pursuit. This extreme produces workaholics; work will eclipse all other important parts of your life: your family, friends, community, and your spirit, leaving you barren.

- *Compassion* taken to extremes becomes obsession. It overshadows the positive vision of an understanding, sensitive, and forgiving heart. This extreme can make you sick when you feel too much empathy for a cause or a person's plight. When you make another person and/or his or her cause more important than your own priorities, perspective, health, well-being, and common sense, you lose balance in your life.
- *Loyalty* taken to extremes becomes blind faith. It overshadows the healthy vision of a faithful, unwavering, and rewarding relationship. This extreme becomes hazardous when you follow commands without question, putting yourself, your life, and others at risk for those who care little about your survival or allegiance.
- *Honesty* taken to extremes becomes destructive. It overshadows the nurturing vision of openness, sincerity, and respect. The extreme becomes destructive when used without regard for other people's feelings or circumstances. When used as self-serving weapons, these indiscrete, vicious opinions offer only malice, not genuine friendship or concern.
- *Respect* taken to extremes becomes fixation. It overshadows the worthy vision of honor, courtesy, and high regard for those you admire. This extreme induces blind loyalty and turns you into a devoted follower,

when you stop asking questions and start following orders. Inhumane and destructive groups, such as the Nazis, gangs, and cults, are examples of respect gone over the edge.

- *Faith* taken to extremes becomes fanatical. It overshadows the spiritual vision of a caring, kind, understanding inner life. This extreme voids spirit, resulting in fear. This fear leads to violence, intolerance, and bigotry.

Can you define how each of these virtues can overshadow their positive vision?

- Education
- Diplomacy
- Power
- Grace
- Gratitude
- Kindness
- Humor
- Duty
- Forgiveness

Do you permit others to define what your virtues are? Only you can determine your own virtues, what they mean, and where they fit into your changing life. The moment you allow others to define your virtues, virtues overshadow visions.

As a dirt farmer, you constantly evaluate and mindfully use your virtues to balance and enrich your life. As you change and grow, your visions and virtues develop with you, helping you to become a stronger, more self-aware person.

Virtues, when in balance with vision, outfit you with all the tools you need to sow the seeds, nurture the crop, and harvest the bounty of a vital, ever-changing life.

Kill the Closest Snake

CHAPTER 7

O n the farm, there is never a lack of chores. Tilling the garden, fertilizing fields, tending animals, fixing farm equipment, and managing finances constantly battle for the top spot on the dirt farmer's priority list.

When countless projects demand your immediate attention, just remember to kill the closest snake.

It's an old story. A farmer walked into his dark barn one evening only to discover the barn crawling with rattlesnakes. Snakes on the floor, snakes under the hay, snakes in the loft, snakes in the rafters. He was trapped, encircled by sidewinders.

There was only one way out. He had to kill the closest snake. Then kill the next one. And the next one. And the next one. Until he reached the door and made it safely outside the barn.

The moral of the story: do first things first, then move on to the next thing, and the next, until you have finished all your chores. You can't weed the garden, milk the cows, and help a neighbor put up a fence all at the same moment. But, if you scratch your tasks off as they come, one at a time, chances are you will finish everything on your list long before you thought you would. If you don't know where to start, you may never start at all. So just start with the first snake.

It is easy for your schedule to become overloaded these days. Meetings, overtime, deadlines, kids, laundry, home-work, and grocery shopping all carry equal weight on the mounting "to do" list. Don't rack your brain trying to decide what should be done first. Just take whatever you see directly in front of you and begin.

My folks taught me to make lists. First, I write down the errands, calls, projects, or chores that I need to take care of. I start at the top and work my way down.

There are agendas, portfolios, and personal planners that can help you keep track of your list of responsibilities. But be careful not to become too distracted by your calen-dar. Some people become so engrossed making lists and planning for what they are going to accomplish, they forget to kill the snakes at hand.

*When in doubt, kill the closest snake and get out
from under that mountain of things to do.*

Anticipate and Participate

CHAPTER 8

Dirt farmers must anticipate everything about their crops before they even begin to sow their fields. They must consider the soil, seeds, compost, plowing, insects, and weather before they decide what crop they're going to plant.

Then they must participate in preparing the soil, setting the seeds, fertilizing the sprouting plants, understanding and watching for insect infestation, and building and monitoring proper irrigation, as they toil toward a bountiful and profitable harvest.

When you anticipate, you plan for a desired outcome then look for all the hidden hurdles and hitches that may stop you from reaching your goal. You participate by executing your plan with educated foresight and dealing with each obstacle as it arises.

Mom and Dad instilled in us a passion for learning, including higher education after high school. They anticipated our future needs for financial and emotional support, in hopes that we would seek further education, whether it was art school, a four-year college, or an advanced degree.

The day we were born, they set up an education fund for

my brother and me. They put money aside each month, and that was only the beginning.

For as long as I can remember they talked about us attending a place of higher learning—usually college—right after high school. I wanted to be a French-speaking marine biologist when I grew up so I could work with Jacques Cousteau. Dad said I would need a college education to do that. What?! That sounded like a lot of work. I just knew I wanted to dive with Jacques; I never considered how I would get there.

Moreover, they provided us with a great example for having an ongoing relationship with our education. Mom and Dad were active in the PTA, knew our teachers by name, and attended every single parent-teacher conference. They reminded us daily how important grades are for getting into college.

I didn't know people had a choice not to further their education after high school. For me, going on to college was as natural as going from junior high to high school.

Again by example, Mom and Dad showed us that learning is a lifelong pursuit. They read books, magazines, and newspapers. Mom loved going to the library, and took us kids with her. My parents loved learning just for fun—like taking classes in Spanish and wine tasting. They read to us. We spent the day at museums and traveling art exhibits. We would go on family learning adventures digging fossils or counting salmon as they swam up the fish ladder.

They anticipated their children going to college and they participated every day by talking about it, teaching us, and encouraging us.

You can anticipate any goal, from losing weight to becoming an engineer to raising the biggest dahlias. You must participate, however, to make that goal a reality. In other words, you can't sit around in your recliner waiting for your opportunity to come knocking.

Anticipation prepares you to create your dream with a plan. Participation applies the plan every day.

Here is how it works:

First, see your dream clearly. Educate yourself about your dream. Research information you need to accomplish your goal. Do you need more or specialized education? Is there someone who can mentor you? How long will it take to become qualified? Most important, are you willing to commit yourself wholeheartedly to your vision?

Second, create a Dirt Farmer Plan of Victory! This will give your vision a concrete blueprint of what you must do.

Include

- Possible obstacles
- A reasonable timetable
- Materials you might require
- Classes you need to take
- A financial budget
- Learning from the mistakes of others
- Finding people for your support system whom you can count on to help you fulfill your dream.

Third, follow your plan through to the end. You will always confront a few obstacles you didn't foresee, but keep going. You might lose some friends along the way who don't understand what you want to accomplish, but keep going. You will sometimes question your own sanity, but keep going. It is worth it!

Granted, there might be a time when you must reevaluate your plan and start over—if you become sick or injured, decide you don't want to achieve your goal any longer, or your plan clearly isn't working. No problem. Create a new plan.

Perhaps you are anticipating buying your first home. You anticipate by thinking about what neighborhood you want to live in, how big a house you need, how much you can afford, and how long it will take to get a down payment together. With your research and information in hand, you can now participate in getting your dream home.

You might have to anticipate serious financial cutbacks. You participate by saving money each paycheck, taking your lunch to work instead of eating out, paying off your credit cards, and only having one latté a day instead of three.

You can dream of a lush green garden but it will never grow unless you find and till suitable soil, plant vegetables or flowers that will grow best in your area, sow the seeds, water, and weed.

It takes hard work and a gentle touch
to produce a healthy, dazzling garden.

Perhaps you want to retire at fifty-five. You have to anticipate this desire long before you turn fifty-four. You can anticipate retirement by investigating how much money you need to retire at fifty-five. Do you want to live in Minnesota or move to Miami? Live in a condo or house? Do you want to continue working after you retire? Start your own business? These are only a few of the considerations you must anticipate when leaving the working world in order to enjoy yourself when you finally retire.

You participate in your retirement step by step. You might decide to put a larger portion of your current income into an IRA. You might want to downsize your dwelling and move into a condo. You may want to spend your retirement as a tour guide in the Grand Canyon—research Arizona!

Wherever and however you want to spend your "golden years" is within your reach, if you anticipate and participate before you get there. Anticipate and participate. Watch your dreams unfold.

⟞⟝

You can brag all you want about how high you expect your crops to be, but if you don't take care of them every day they will just burn up and blow away.

Take the First Circus

CHAPTER 9

Dirt farmers work with what is right in front of them: equipment, soil, water, and weather.

They don't have time to waste waiting or dreaming of something better to come along to help them run the farm.

Taking the first circus is a story about a little boy named Bobby. Bobby was excited about the circus coming to his small Nebraska town. The circus was full of lions, clowns, and people who flew out of cannons. Bobby and his friends were thrilled. They could hardly wait to see the show under the big top.

One day Bobby heard there was going to be yet another circus setting up tents at the county fair grounds just one week after the first circus performed. Rumor had it the second circus was even better than the first. It was supposed to have elephants and giraffes, plus a man who ate fire. Bobby decided that he would skip the first circus and go to the second circus instead.

His friends skittered by him excited as they headed to the circus that was already in town. But that was nothing compared to their amazement after seeing the show! They told Bobby every thrilling detail.

One small problem arose. The second circus never came to town. Word had it they went broke. All their performers and animals joined the first circus in the next city, including the man who ate fire.

Poor Bobby. He was left with only the fantastic stories about the lions, tigers, and the man flying out of a cannon.

Bobby could have gone to the first circus, which was definitely going to happen, or wait for the second circus, which turned out to be only an entertaining rumor. If he had gone to the first circus with his friends, he could have always returned to see the second big top when it finally came to town. If you pass up one definite opportunity to wait for another one that is based on speculation, hearsay, or wishful thinking you might miss out on the event altogether.

*Sell your harvest to the buyer who is ready
to make the deal, is willing to pay the best price,
and has the cash in hand.*

Don't save your bounty for the illusive, wealthy customer who may never show up, because in the end you will be left with your pockets empty and your crops still waiting to be sold.

Have you ever driven into a mall parking lot and spied an empty parking space right in front of you? You figure if you found that one so quickly, then there must be another one closer to the entrance. So you pass that space up and drive on looking for a space closer to the door. Then you spend the next forty-five minutes driving around looking for another place to park, since the space you originally saw has now been taken. If you grab the first empty slot you see, you'll be cruising the mall in no time.

Maybe you are looking for a new job. You've interviewed with several companies. You have one firm offer and two prospects that look good, but they offer nothing in writing. What do you do?

You have to make a choice. You can put off making a decision about the concrete offer and wait to see what else might come through—but that might cost you that job. On the other hand, if the job offered has the salary, the benefits, and the advancement opportunities you want—don't hesitate, take it!

You can take the first circus, root out firm dates for the second extravaganza, or you can just wait it out and see what happens, risking everything. Caution and skepticism are healthy when investigating opportunities. You don't want to jump on something that looks too good just because it was offered. And you don't have to settle for anything that isn't right. Take action! You can't keep waiting for something better or you'll be waiting forever. When you are looking for an apartment to rent, a house to buy, a car to purchase, or a space to lease, don't settle for something less than you want, but don't hesitate to the point that the choice will be made for you.

Don't wait for the circus to pass you by.
Seize opportunities!
Don't wait around for the circus that never comes.

*Stop Cussing the Mule and
Load the Wagon*

CHAPTER 10

O n the farm, there are always dirty jobs that no one is
eager to do. Replacing irrigation pipes in the mud,
dunging out the barn, or chopping firewood in a
downpour are duties that can't be avoided.

Simple errands, important duties, and special projects
can stack up in a hurry. Sometimes you lock horns with a
daily chore or an upcoming project that, without a doubt,
you absolutely, positively don't want to tackle.

When you run up against these tasks, you have to stop
cussing the mule and start loading the wagon. In other
words, stop fussing and start working.

Your life is full of must do's, gotta do's, and should do's.
It is easy to push projects aside until time runs out and then
you have to do them, like it or not.

"Cussing the mule" is the excuses we find not to get
started on the job in front of us. You might be too tired to do
the laundry. Perhaps you just aren't inspired to write that
thank-you note. Maybe you are nervous about making that
sales call. Or you'll just put it off until tomorrow when you
have more time.

Don't let these tasks get the better of you. Stop thinking

up reasons why you can't and just get started. If you are staring at the mountain of paper on your desk that stares back, then it's time to stop cussing the mule and pull out the paper shredder or file them in their new home! If you have no underwear for the next day, you might stop cussing the mule and load the washing machine. If you have no business appointments for the upcoming week, you better stop cussing the mule and pick up the phone. If you have no idea where to start on your twenty-five-page term paper, stop cussing the mule and pick up your pencil.

The more time you spend thinking of reasons why you can't begin a task, the bigger torture it becomes to do it and the longer it will take to finish it. The garden won't wait for water, animals can't wait for feed, and the crops won't wait until you've cleared your schedule to harvest them.

Put the mule out to pasture and bring him back when the wagon is full and ready to go.

Learning Is a Family Business

CHAPTER 11

A dirt farmer adds fertilizer to keep her pasture healthy
and help it grow stronger faster.

S he mixes up organic materials and spreads them out on the field to enrich the soil. Her hard work helps create a plentiful harvest. Just as compost, minerals, and bone meal nourish the soil, learning feeds the mind. Learning is fertilizer for your life.

Learning is more than just sitting in a classroom trying to figure out the hypotenuse of a triangle. Learning is about spending time with your family discovering something new together.

Learning was our family business. No question was too strange, no idea too weird, no topic out of bounds. If we wanted to know something, Mom and Dad would help us investigate until we found an answer.

They prompted our desire to learn more. We dug fossils in the deserts of eastern Oregon, we fished for steelhead on the Oregon Coast, and we attended the first Wildlife Federation Conference in the Rocky Mountains. We did all this as a family.

Dad always carried books on birds and geology and a pair of binoculars in the car. He would pull our wood-sided station wagon off the road in a flourish of dust, and we would take turns peering through the binoculars to watch a hawk make lazy circles in the sky or check out a layered rock formation.

Because Mom and Dad actively pursued their passion for learning, I developed it too. I devour books with glee, take classes just for fun, and dive into continuing education because it challenges me.

You can't ignore one crop in favor of another or both will suffer.

My parents took us on wonderful adventures but never forgot that we had to succeed in school too.

But there were problems. Mom and Dad were horrified when they realized I had been promoted through third grade without being able to read. That summer they hired a tutor, drafting a neighboring high-school girl to read with me every day after lunch. I read for one hour, five days a week during the entire summer. I learned to read and to love it.

Although I fiercely complained when I had to come in from playing with my friends, Vicky made reading fun. We read the biography of Louis Braille and the story of Helen Keller. Reading each chapter out loud, Vicky made sure I understood everything I read. It was hard work that summer, but it was worth it. My world opened because my parents made my learning a family business.

When learning is a family affair it moves beyond school boundaries and into your daily life. When you discover you can learn anytime, anywhere, it becomes fun.

I learned manners from going out to dinner with my mother. I learned that there were consequences to my actions when I didn't tell the truth. I learned that my parents still loved me even when I made a mistake.

A lifelong love of learning is a great gift to pass on.
When learning becomes a family business,
the profits soar.

The Deeper the Roots,
the Stronger the Tree

CHAPTER 12

A dirt farmer relies on her apple trees for many things. They provide shade from the hot sun for both farmer and cow, fruit for applesauce and pies, and a place to hang her hammock.

The apple trees can only provide these things if they are strong and healthy. They remain hearty when their roots tap into the nourishing soil and are expanded far and wide, giving the trees a rock solid footing.

Without this strong underground foundation, the trees would collapse under the weight of the hammock, there would be no leaves for shade, and there would be no fruit for Thanksgiving pies.

Your roots are the people in your life who sustain and support you, from your friends to your family to other people in your community. When your roots run deep you have many people to call on when you need help.

Before there were community watch programs, neighbors looked out for one another. You knew who your neighbors were and you took care of each other. If your barn blew down, everyone banded together to build a new one. If your children had measles, your neighbors brought over chicken soup for mother and child. If you were away on vacation, you could count on your friends and neighbors to feed your cat, water your plants, and protect your home.

A tree's roots spread out, intermingling with neighboring trees, shrubs, and plants, lending strength, kinship, and balance to all.

I grew up on a street that was the most direct route to the local hamburger joint. It was the place to hang out and be cool, much as the mall is today. Teenagers raced their hot rods at breakneck speed up the street, much to the alarm of the neighborhood parents. With so many little kids running around, they were afraid someone would get hit.

The parents united to find a solution. Each homeowner placed a 4×4 piece of lumber on the street in front of his or her house. They created the first homegrown speed bumps.

At first, the teenagers tossed the logs aside. Then they

drove over them very slowly, which doesn't really work for drag racing. Ultimately, they simply found another route to the burger stand. Problem solved, thanks to the interwoven roots of the neighborhood.

Building strong, deep roots takes time and genuine effort.

You have almost limitless choices to spread your roots, if you're willing to put yourself out into the world.

You can sign your children up at the local pool, YMCA or YWCA, to take swimming lessons, and meet other parents as you enjoy watching your kids together from the stands. If you feel like extending your roots in a creative way, audition for a local play, or you can offer to paint the sets or create the costumes for the next production. If your need-to-help roots are calling for expansion, volunteer at an animal shelter or become a mentor to a child who could really use your attention and wisdom. The stronger you make your ties to the community, the stronger both you and your community become.

My dad's roots stretched far and wide. He was on a first-name basis with my high-school principal and all of my teachers. I knew that if I ever dared to skip school I would be caught in a heartbeat. So I never did.

He knew just the right person to call when my brother's little league baseball teams were looking for a "popcorn" wagon to sell coffee, hotdogs, and snow cones at the games to raise money. After they purchased a used bread truck, Dad found plumbers who donated their skills and material and carpenters who built shelves, and he even knew an artist, who painted the logo in bright colors on the side of the wagon.

Dad knew a businessman who sold used automobile engines in Japan. He asked my dad if he knew anyone who spoke fluent Japanese and was well versed in the customs. It just so happens that one of my brother's closest friends was in Japan at the same time looking for a job. Dad connected these two men, and both found just the person they had been seeking. Dad's roots stretched so wide, they grew around the world!

Call it networking, being neighborly, sharing the wealth, or being community minded, but it boils down to one thing: being fully rooted in your life.

You can't bring in the harvest all by yourself.

As your roots become strong, deep, and healthy you can overcome hurdles and accomplish seemingly impossible tasks.

*There is nothing too far from your reach
when your roots extend from your heart.*

No Point Digging a Sinkhole

CHAPTER 13

T he city slicker was digging like crazy in his yard. His shovel cut into the ground at a frightening speed, creating a vast crater. A mound of earth was piled barn high, while the hole got wider and deeper.

The dirt farmer stopped by to investigate the new mountain range, when the city slicker popped up from the hole and complained about how hard he was working and that it wasn't doing any good. The dirt farmer walked to the edge of the gaping crevice, peered over the side, and said, "That's because you're digging a sinkhole."

The funny thing about digging a sinkhole is that you may look busy, but the truth is you're just spinning your wheels. A sinkhole may look like a hole, but in reality it serves no purpose. The hole is not a well for drinking water, it's not an irrigation line, and it's not a fence post hole. In fact, a sinkhole is dangerous because, as the bottom drops out, it consumes everything in its neighborhood. In short, a sinkhole is a hazard to your family, your animals, and your life.

Are you digging sinkholes in your life? Time is too precious to squander becoming an expert in things that don't benefit you, personally or professionally.

LeeAnn loved being on the cutting edge of fashion and she spent long hours trying to stay one step ahead of the crowd. She became a voracious shopper on a limited budget. She spent her time and money combing trendy shops, discount department stores, and mall clothing outlets to buy the latest fashions. She knew what day discount stores received new merchandise and when the newest seasons knockoffs would arrive at the boutiques, and she marked her calendar with the dates of upscale department store supersales.

She knew how to spot flaws, nicks, and irregulars to garner further discounts. She gained all the skills of a professional stylist. Filling up her closets with new clothes was not just her favorite hobby; it was a way of life.

LeeAnn may have been a gifted bargain hunter, but she couldn't afford her lavish lifestyle. Being a fashion plate was costing her more than money. She became so deeply in debt that she couldn't sleep. She had more than ten credit cards maxed out; her salary was barely enough to cover the minimum payments. She could no longer keep her financial head above water.

LeeAnn may have looked stunning, but she was literally drowning in debt. She received threatening phone calls from collection agencies, was handed an eviction notice because her rent was constantly overdue, and became ill from all the stress brought on by this financial nightmare. Her credit and her health were in ruins.

Finally, realizing she could no longer live with her debts, she cut up all her credit cards, went to a nonprofit organization called Consumer Credit Counseling, and changed the priorities in her life. Now she spends her money paying down her debt. She might no longer be a fashion trendsetter, but she now sleeps at night and isn't terrified to answer her phone.

Are you spending your time perfecting skills that enrich your life? Or are you digging sinkholes that waste or even destroy it? Only you can know which is which.

Are you spending every weekend at the driving range improving your swing at the expense of cheering your daughter on to victory at her ball game? Do you have the highest score ever recorded for a video game, but never talk to your wife? Are you spending hours training and grooming your prizewinning pedigree pups but not helping your husband plan your son's birthday party? Do you have a perfectly organized home office with color-coded file folders, stacking racks full of brochures, and a matching in/out basket, but not have any sales appointments scheduled for the upcoming month?

Roy wanted to learn everything he could about the Internet so he could make a career change. He came home from work every night, hopped on the computer, and disappeared for hours behind his glowing computer screen, surfing the net.

He researched vacation destinations, stocks he would like to buy, and the latest in fuzzy car seat covers. Roy taught himself how to download music and software from the Web, then bought more powerful hardware and picked up more RAM to run all his goodies. He learned shortcuts through the maze of Web sites, applied the information he reaped from different sources, and became extremely proficient in Web design. In fact, Roy thought he had learned enough that he could actually change careers.

The only problem with Roy's increasing Web savvy was that he had a wife and two kids who rarely saw him anymore. He went to work at 8:00 AM, returned home around 5:30 PM, plopped his briefcase down, and scurried into the den. He came up for air and ate dinner with the family, but vanished again as soon as he had gulped down his last bite.

He may have been gaining great new skills at the computer, but it was at the expense of the rest of his life. He had no relationship to speak of with his children, and his marriage was hanging on by a tattered modem connection.

One afternoon Roy's wife Terri unplugged the computer, boxed it up, and took it over to her mother's house for safekeeping. Terri called a family meeting. The kids told Roy how much they missed him helping them with their homework. Terri let him know that their marriage was in big trouble and changes had to be made or they would be heading for divorce court. Roy wasn't aware how much his new passion affected his family, but he understood things had to change.

Roy is now a full-time Web designer. He pursues his enthusiasm for the Internet during business hours and keeps his free time available to help with homework.

Improving yourself and increasing your skills or knowledge are noble callings as long as they are not at the expense of the rest of your life. Spend your time, energy, and money in pursuit of something that ultimately enhances your life. Take classes that will further your career, help you to finish school, or turn your hobby into a full-time profession. Pursue your passion with gusto, but don't forget the people who count on you or your daily responsibilities.

Spend your time in pursuit of skills that enhance your life and give you pleasure but don't let them become a stumbling block.

Don't waste time digging a sinkhole; it only makes you hot and sweaty, and in the end you don't get anywhere.

Stand Your Ground or
Lose Your Footing

CHAPTER 14

When gale force winds and driving rains hit the dirt farm, cherry trees only stand a chance of surviving if they are rooted firmly in the ground.

Your beliefs are like the roots of the cherry tree.
They form your foundation, supporting
the diverse branches of your life.

They nourish you in times of spiritual famine and strengthen you when you face stormy arguments. Your beliefs make you unique in the world. Beliefs can be as complicated as how you interpret God or as simple as the notion that wearing white shoes after Labor Day is a fashion sin.

When growing roots run into a rock or hard-packed soil, they simply change direction and move around it. Just as roots adjust their routes, your convictions and beliefs can also change direction in order to nourish your body and soul. Not only can your beliefs change, but they do daily. The battles you were willing to wage in high school are far different from the crusades you are willing to take on as an adult.

Roots feed the tree, just as beliefs feed your spirit. If roots are diseased with fear, hatred, ignorance, or destructive behavior, the tree weakens and dies. It will blow over with a gentle gust.

Hold fast to your beliefs. They give you confidence in the face of conflict and a solid structure to grasp when you're standing on shaky ground.

In a crowded garden full of trees, shrubs, and flowers, roots of every kind intermingle. They form a bond where all the roots are equally protected against outside harm. If they don't accommodate each other, the balance is lost, and a single, ravenous tree can choke out and devour everything surrounding it. There are those who would like to choke out your beliefs and replace them with their own. But in the cooperative garden, all roots lend strength and support to maintain a healthy balance and help all plants flourish. This also prevents destructive roots from gaining a foothold in the garden.

One summer Sunday Carolynn made dinner for her family and visiting in-laws. After dinner, as they sat around the table, with her two young daughters, her father-in-law let loose with a string of racial slurs. Carolynn was furious, but waited until the girls left the table to talk to her disrespectful father-in-law.

Carolynn politely asked him to refrain from making racist comments in front of her and her children. She didn't ask him to change his beliefs, just not to express them in front of her family. Her father-in-law insisted she was overreacting and chastised her for making such a big deal out of it. Carolynn calmly reiterated that she did not want him to do it again.

Her father-in-law stood up, pushed back his chair, thanked her for dinner, and left. He didn't speak to Carolynn or anyone in her family for six months. He didn't send birthday cards to his granddaughters, he didn't attend holiday gatherings, and he refused to take her phone calls.

Carolynn stood her ground. There was no way she was going to allow offensive, bigoted remarks in her home, especially in front of her children. Although it was difficult, she knew it was the right thing to do for herself and her family.

Your beliefs are the ideas that help you determine right from wrong, the moral principles that give you strength when you are faced with adversity, and the conviction to stand up against injustice when you see it.

Everyone has a right to his or her own beliefs, and no two people believe exactly the same about everything. So what will you do when faced with someone who says something or takes action that disparages, belittles, or ignores your beliefs?

It depends. There are some battles you will never win, so why bother trying? Debating politics, religion, and some sports teams can get you in trouble. You may find yourself either preaching to the converted or shoveling sand against the tide.

There are times, however, when you must stand firm and hold your ground. If you see injustice, step in, even if it is simply to object. If you witness abusive behavior, take action, even if it is only to call the police. If you hear someone make racist, sexist, or generally harassing remarks, speak up, even if only to ask why he would say something like that. He may never change, but by taking positive action based on your beliefs you have shed light on his behavior and made him accountable.

Other unchecked influences can also be destructive. You lose your footing when you allow outside, contrived messages to erode your beliefs. Media, advertising, propaganda, your peers, and sometimes even your family try to chop away at your roots. If you allow that to happen your confidence can wither.

Choose your battles carefully. By speaking up or taking reasonable action, you can be the vital, sturdy cherry tree, leaning with the blustery winds, doing no damage to you or yours. You can maintain your beliefs without imposing them on others, not allowing others to force their beliefs on you or letting others suffer unnecessarily.

Stand firm. Your beliefs, ideas, and opinions are uniquely yours. They make you a firmly rooted, solid force in a stormy world. No one else sees the world exactly as you do. Your thoughts matter.

Speak your mind. Stand your ground. Hold tight to your footing. Or you may simply wash away.

Push the Cows, Pull the Cows

CHAPTER 15

When it is time to load up the cows to take them to market, the dirt farmer calls in reinforcements. The cows have to be moved into the corral, hastened down the shoot, loaded on the truck, and boarded up for their journey.

To run this gauntlet smoothly requires a team effort. One person has to push the cows toward the corral by slapping them on the backside, others have to keep pulling them through the course from the front side, and still other intrepid cowhands have to stand by just in case one jumpy cow makes a break for it through the fence.

It takes a dedicated team to get cows to market. A team is a group of people striving toward a common end. They must work together or the job never gets done.

On most teams, you have the leader who assigns the jobs, supervises the work, and is usually the last one to call it a night. A team trooper takes direction and works with the leader to get the job done well and in good time.

And, unfortunately, on every team there always seems to be a complainer. The complainer doesn't take direction; he gripes while others sweat, and is the first to leave when the sun dips below the horizon. The complainer usually doesn't have a job for long.

My mom and dad are leaders. When I was growing up, they volunteered to head up almost everything involving us kids. Mom was the president of the PTA; my parents worked together to raise money for our sports and school activities, and chaperoned our school dances. (That's one activity I wish they would not have volunteered for!)

When it came time for the barbecue fund-raiser, Mom, Dad, and two more couples stepped up to run the show and plan the event. They had to get Park Department permits, scrounge up tables, track down barbecues, and, of course, round up the vittles. They were the leaders of the pack.

As leaders, they had to find helpers, parents who could only work the day of the big barbecue. These troopers cooked long hours over flaming briquettes, staffed the condiment station, made sure there was enough ice for the lemonade, and were willing to run to the store down the road at a moment's notice. At the last minute, one trooper could not work the day of the event, but to show his support he bought and ate seven hamburgers. He said it was the least he could do for such a good cause.

As the barbecue proceeded smoothly, the complainers, whom we called the grumblers, lurked nearby looking for any sign of trouble. During the planning sessions, the grumblers would condescendingly point out all the reasons the fundraiser would fail. Permits would be hard to get, no one would pay $3.50 for a hamburger, the whole undertaking would be messy and too hard to clean up. The leaders pursued it anyway.

The grumblers didn't have time to help with the event, but they did show up long enough to criticize the tables, condiments, buns, napkins, and pickles. Despite the admonishments of the self-righteous grumblers, the barbecue was a smashing financial hit.

After the event, leaders and troopers alike cleaned the park, hauled away the barbecue grills, scrubbed and removed the tables, and polished off the last potato chip. As they congratulated each other on a job well done, the grumblers were nowhere to be seen.

Every organization, business, family, and farm needs a leader. Someone who can plan, schedule, coordinate, and direct meetings, events, vacations, and active lives. Leaders inspire others and get things rolling.

Every group also needs followers. People who carry out instructions and work hard so that the meetings, events, and vacations run smoothly.

It's helpful for someone to make constructive suggestions so the group can create positive solutions for any activity. That's not the grumbler. The grumbler just tells you a project simply "can't be done." The grumbler is a complainer who finds only the flaws in your plan or who points out the insurmountable hurdles at every step. These people don't help get things done; they only get in the way.

Leaders can be followers too!

Roles change. One day you might be the leader, the next day the follower. Both are important roles in getting things accomplished.

You might be a leader at your child's school by being an active member of the PTA and a follower at your church by bringing cookies to a tea. You might be an assistant helping to raise money to build a new hospital wing, then become the family leader, planning a spring break vacation. There are even times when you might volunteer to lead a campaign, then realize that it takes more time than you originally thought, so you demote yourself and become a trusty follower.

You don't have to be the kink in the rope. Anyone can point out problems, but it takes a strong person to help find solutions. If you see problems in the planning stages, don't just grumble; pitch in and help find an answer. Encourage brainstorming and problem solving. If you see the need for one more worker, raise your hand and join the fun, recommend someone else, or try to recruit an additional trooper. Extend yourself and belong, don't sit in the back and complain.

⬤▬▬

It makes no difference if you are a leader or a follower; when the harvest is finished and safely tucked away in the barn, everyone on the team enjoys the celebration.

Every Day Is a Gift

CHAPTER 16

The dirt farmer takes advantage of every plant, tree, shrub, flower, and stalk because the growing season is gone before you know it.

There are three months in spring for seeds to carefully emerge from the safety of the winter ground and sprout tender shoots that catch the sun. There are only three summer months for plants to develop full height, flourish, and multiply before fall arrives with cool, crisp evenings signaling an end to the life cycle.

We sprout as innocent babies in the spring of our lives, while others carefully protect and nourish us as we grow. We move on into summer still growing, trying to gain maturity and insight, thinking we will live forever. As fall dawns, we have reached our full height, seen friends and family fall along the way, maintaining a hope that death will not find us. As winter glides into our lives, our branches shrink, and we watch others pass underground waiting for spring to arrive again. Every day is a gift because like the growing season, our lives are over before we know it.

When I was six, Dad was diagnosed with terminal cancer and told he would die in six months. From that moment, nothing was more important to him than spending each second with his wife and children. We spent time on the weekends running around the Oregon coast, chasing kites, and laughing until tears streamed down our faces. Dad wanted to create joyous memories for his family, something for us to hold onto when he passed.

Thankfully, Dad found out that he had been misdiagnosed. He had a rare blood disorder, a treatable condition—not cancer. Not only was he going to live, but he still has many more years to spend with his family.

When Dad thought he was dying, working fifteen hours a day, six days a week, and being on the road for weeks at a time just didn't seem as important anymore. Making a living mattered, but nothing was more significant to him than his family. He learned that every day he spent with the people he loved was a treasure.

If you become sick with a serious illness or suffer through a traumatic event, it opens your eyes to just how short and precious life truly is. When you are reminded that every day is a gift and that it can be gone in a heartbeat, living becomes about today. You can't take a second for granted; it might disappear.

It is easy to forget life is short when you have a list of

worries a mile long and tasks that don't want to wait. Bills need to be paid, grass needs to be mowed, the deadline for your marketing report is looming, and the school Halloween party needs clothes for the ghouls and goblins. Don't wait for a serious illness, the death of a friend, or a fatal accident to scare you back to living, back to understanding what is really important.

Chores will wait; life won't.

It is the little things that matter most: the nights that you tuck your son into bed, wish him sweet dreams, and kiss him tenderly good night. Seeing your daughter dressed in pink ruffles, prancing to Swan Lake, grinning from ear to ear but not keeping time with the other dancers. Holding your mom's hand as you walk through your favorite antique flea market, arguing over whose fried chicken is better. The moment you turn to see your father's face when you say "I do." Or smiling when your parents finally accept and understand that you may never officially get married to the love of your life.

When you know that every day is a gift, the celebration of your life is never ending. Tell your family and friends that you love them. Take time to cherish the people, places, animals, and things that make your life so special and uniquely yours.

Feed Yourself

CHAPTER 17

A dirt farmer works hard every day of the year. She tends the fields, feeds the animals, manages the farm finances, and takes care of her family.

The daily list of duties is long and constantly growing, but a dirt farmer knows that she must also schedule time to feed herself—mind, body, and spirit—so she can handle the challenges, stresses, and joys she faces every day.

Her body is strong, her mind is sharp, and her spirit and intuition guide her.

If, however, she doesn't take care of her complete self, the dirt farmer will not be able to effectively deal with all the pressures placed on her shoulders.

It is important to balance the care of your body, mind, and spirit. If you tend to only one element and ignore the others, you create an imbalance that results in a lopsided life. For example, if you focus only on feeding and exercising your body, while neglecting your mind, the result is a strong physical presence, but an unexercised mind. If you concentrate on your spirituality alone, the physical body will erode, leaving your "temple" to decay. And if you only feed your mind, forsaking your spirituality and body, you will be smart as a whip, but no one will want to be around you. Balance is the key to experiencing your life to its fullest potential.

As a successful partner in a T-shirt company, Alexis typically spends twelve hours a day, Monday through Friday, in her office, then happily exhausts most weekends selling shirts at street fairs. She goes to the gym and works out to keep her body in shape, but she's so focused on the success of her business that she forgets to eat and never gets enough sleep. She says she loves her frantic life, but every time she takes a vacation, she gets sick.

She takes care of her company, her husband, her business partner, and her figure, but she neglects the rest of herself. She is wound tighter than a toy airplane's rubber band, and when she finally lets her guard down, her body collapses. She has a choice to make: to continue on her physically exhausting roller-coaster lifestyle until a serious illness forces her to slow down for good or to take time to care for herself. Her body is sending her clear messages, but it is up to her to listen.

To keep your body strong you must feed it well. It needs fresh food, lots of water, and balanced nutrition. You know how good you feel when you eat right. Exercise is another critical element that will keep you in motion. You don't have to spend two hours in the gym every day to be in shape. Take twenty-minute walks around your neighborhood to get you moving and breathing deeply. This can also help clear your mind of unwanted noise.

The most overlooked aspect of caring for your body is rest. This is your regenerative state. Mom always told me to go to bed when I was tired regardless of the time. Now I am known to turn out my light at 8:00 PM if my fanny is dragging. I have no shame when it comes to getting sleep, because when I'm tired I am terrible to deal with. Without enough sleep, we all become tall two-year-olds. We're grouchy and impatient; we distort the words and actions of others and suffer diminished physical, emotional, and mental responses—leaving us thoroughly impaired. Most people I know don't get enough sleep. Do you?

The last aspect of feeding all three—body, mind, and spirit—is quiet solitude. This means no television, no radio, no telephone, no newspaper, and no computer. Nothing to distract you from spending a few silent moments with your thoughts and emotions. Listen. Hear what your body is telling you. Does something hurt? Do you feel tired? Your body will tell you what it needs if you pay attention to its silent and sometimes painful messages.

Do you get sick when you go on vacation? When you don't get enough sleep are you more prone to accidents? It is amazing how you can put your stress into perspective when you stop and be quiet for just five minutes. Breathe. Enjoy a few minutes devoted to you and only you. This is as important as what you eat.

Feed your mind. Nourish it with challenges, stimulation, and rest.

Henry is ninety-plus years young. He swims every day, keeping his body in tremendous shape. And to keep his mind sharp and alert he writes one limerick every morning. He enjoys the challenge of matching rhymes and syllables, meter and story. Henry keeps his mind as fit as he keeps his body.

Keep your mind nimble by avoiding routine or getting mired in mundane activities. Spice up your drive home from work by taking a different route. It's more interesting if you aren't familiar with every single traffic light or stop sign. Discover something new about your neighborhood or your city. Pick out a book different from your favorite genre. If you love romance novels, choose an adventure or detective story instead. Buy a language tape and listen to it in your car. Before you know it you will *habla Español.*

Finally, you need to feed your spirit.

As with your physical body and emotional, intellectual mind, you feed your inner self when you become still. These silent, introspective moments help you define who you are and where you fit in the world.

When you treat your spirit with gentle care and nourish it with sweeping sunrises, the hushed breathing of a sleeping child, or a loving embrace of your favorite furry friend, you are fully connected to life.

When your spirit is satisfied, you can cope with the shifting image of who you are and where you belong. Your fears diminish, and you know you are not alone. When you listen to your inner voice, you are able to maneuver through the obstacles that present themselves.

When your spirit is starving, it leads to disconnection, depression, fear, and the inability to make sense of a volatile world. Some kind of spiritual nourishment is a necessity if you are to flourish.

Tend your mind, feed your body, and nourish your spirit as if they are the most important things on your "to-do" list. Put them on your daily planner. When you don't take care of your whole self—mind, body, and spirit—your plate is empty.

You can't feed others if you are starving. But, when you care for yourself, your own plate becomes full, and then you can reach out and feed the world because you have something to share.

Let Anger Fix the Fence

CHAPTER 18

When the neighbor's cows get loose and wander on over to your field to munch your tender grass for the fifth time, getting riled up and yelling at the cows won't do any good. Cows don't care if you are angry; they're just looking for greener pastures and tastier turf. Don't get mad at your neighbors either. Take action. Fix the fence.

Let the energy brought on by your anger motivate you to quit bitching and get to work. Mend the fence.

Anger can spur you to positive action or it can destroy your life. It's too late to save your grass after the cows have snacked on your field, so let your anger incite you to action, and you'll mend your fence in half the time. Put your energy from being pissed off to good use.

If you don't put your anger to work for you, it will only fester and turn into resentment, and become harmful. Don't allow anger to turn into injury for you or anyone else.

When Bernie graduated from high school after being picked on relentlessly, he vowed he was going to come back and "show them." His anger motivated him to create a successful career, as an adult. He went to a prestigious university, received his engineering degree, and became a prosperous aviation designer.

His accomplishments were the positive outcome of his anger. But there was a negative side to Bernie's unresolved bitterness. When he made an appearance at his ten-year high-school reunion, he couldn't wait to prove to his tormentors how successful he had become. He wanted to rub it in their faces. He drove an expensive car to the gathering, wore a designer suit to dinner, and talked loudly about his money, travels, women, condo, and cars.

He may have been materially successful, but he was still lugging around all those years of resentment. He was trapped in the past, with the mind of a young, embittered victim. This is the tragic outcome of keeping anger alive.

Whether it's bad drivers, rude clerks, long lines at the post office, taxes, horrendous traffic, or your neighbor's dog barking at all hours, how do you deal with your anger? Make it work for you.

- If you see a reckless driver terrorizing motorists, get mad and take action. Write down the license number, call 911, and report the driver. If enough people report road-raging drivers, they will be held accountable for their behavior. Your actions do make a difference.

- If you receive terrible service or you are waiting forever for your food in a restaurant, stewing about it won't satisfy your anger. Ask to speak with the manager and complain right on the spot. Write a complaint on the back of the bill or write a letter to the owners when you get home.
- If you witness animal abuse, don't mull over all the things you could have done to save the animal later, do something when you see it. You can confront the abuser, call 911 for help, or alert animal control and swear out a formal complaint. Animal shelters do not ordinarily kill abused animals they rescue. They warn abusive owners or put the pets up for adoption.
- If you receive uninvited sales phone calls after asking the repeat offenders to take you off their list, cursing the phone every time it rings won't make them stop. Tell them you want to be taken off their list. Write the company and complain to your state attorney general.

Work out your anger as it comes up. Don't let the fire in your eyes have a chance to root into your heart. Allow anger to motivate you, but don't let it destroy you. There is always a solution out there, waiting to be found; you just have to have the courage, cool head, and determination to find it.

When I opened my credit card bill one day, I noticed a $50 charge that didn't look familiar. I racked my brain to figure out what this charge could be, then became angry, believing I had been scammed. Keeping my anger in check, I immediately called the credit card company to get detailed information regarding the charge. I calmly assured the representative that I hadn't bought anything from the business listed on my account.

The customer service representative on the phone was polite and very helpful. She told me to write a letter stating that I questioned a charge on my bill. They would then investigate the charge. In the meantime, they would remove the charge from my bill.

As it turns out, my suspicions were correct. It was a mistake, and I was never billed. Taking action instead of fuming saved me $50. Do you carefully check your credit card bills?

Anything is possible when you turn your anger into positive action. You can change government policies, the method you use to help your business succeed, the manner in which your family deals with problems, and the style in which you handle life's challenges.

No point yelling at the cows for being cows or holding a grudge against your neighbor. Step back, locate the hole, and figure out the best way to fix it. Then mend the fence.

Life's Too Short to Take Serious

CHAPTER 19

Something is always breaking, clogging, backfiring, or just plain not working on the farm. That's why a dirt farmer always carries a toolbox in his pickup, a sense of humor in his heart, and the knowledge that life is too short to take serious.

L ife is about laughter, love, good memories, and taking challenges in stride. It is easy to lose sight of that when the kids are screaming, you're late for a crucial meeting, or there is barely enough money to cover rent and food.

Stuck in traffic? Stop. Shake out your sense of humor, slap on a grin, and laugh a little. It will help you find a cure for what ails you.

It is easy to remember life is too short when you hear about a plane crash that kills everyone on board. But do you remember that life is too short when the cable goes out during the ninth inning of a tied game between your favorite baseball team and their toughest rival?

My dad found himself making a life-and-death issue of

the University of Oregon football team's win/loss record. He would jump up and down in his seat at the stadium, yell, red-faced, at the officials, and be flooded with excitement when they won.

But he was thoroughly devastated when they lost. He would rehash each game over and over as he waited expectantly for the next one. When it came to his favorite college football team, he forgot that life is too short to take serious.

In the off-season, he fell into a postseason stupor. When he finally snapped out of his fanatical immersion, he realized he was exhausted. He had wasted too much time and energy on an outcome about which he could do absolutely nothing.

He was so upset that he had lost his perspective; he stopped watching college football for years. Although some would argue otherwise, football is only a game. Dad was making it a matter of far too much importance. Today Dad buys tickets for home games, but he knows that if his team loses, they will play again next year.

When you are flinging your golf clubs across the greens and into water hazards, endangering flora and fauna, do you realize that life is too short to take serious? When the official makes a bad call at your child's hockey game, and you yell obscenities in front of other children, do you realize that life is too short to take serious? When your computer crashes and you haven't backed up your new files, will you recall that life is too short to take serious?

When you are stuck in traffic that seems to stretch for miles, will you take a deep breath and realize that life is too short to take serious?

There will always be frustrating challenges that you must face head-on. But you can choose how to tackle them. Which do you prefer—humor or tears?

Avoid spending your precious moments on people, activities, or careers that don't ultimately bring you joy and satisfaction. Take hurdles in stride, and laugh every chance you get. After all, life is too short to take serious.

When your tractor breaks down right in the middle of haying, you can stomp around, shaking your fist at the darn thing or you can decide that this would be a good time for a short coffee break before returning to repair the problem.

Giving Is Receiving

CHAPTER 20

A dirt farmer takes care of his neighborhood. If the farmer down the road needs help hooking up a generator, the dirt farmer drops by with his toolbox, ready to lend a hand. If a local family is having a rough year, a dirt farmer and her family stop by with a pickup truck full of firewood and boxes of homemade applesauce and sausages.

A dirt farmer takes care of his community because
it is the right thing to do and because one day
he might need a little help, too.

Giving is receiving when your generosity of heart or pocketbook makes you feel pleased and satisfied, and when you feel no need to be recognized for those efforts. You can be motivated to give because it is the right thing to do, because you want to share your bounty, because you hope to pass on helpful information, or because that's simply who you are. Any reason you wish to give of yourself is good as long as you don't expect anything in return.

If you feel you "have" to give something, that is not giving. That's paying taxes.

Giving is about the joyous feeling you experience, not about going into debt. It is about helping when you don't have to, not because it is company policy.

Dad was driving through a bustling downtown street in Portland, Oregon, when he saw a frightened man on the street blowing a little red plastic whistle. Dad pulled over to the curb, disregarding the No Parking signs, and jumped out to see what was wrong.

As it turns out, the man was blind. He blew his whistle to attract help. He was lost and terrified. He couldn't find his bus, and no one had bothered to stop to help him find his way home.

Angry drivers honked at Dad's illegally parked car while he walked this gentle man to his bus stop. Dad gladly gave three minutes of his time to help someone in distress. Doing a good deed can be such a wonderful source of satisfaction. The true gift of giving is how good it makes you feel. If you are lonely and feeling disconnected from your life, volunteer at a day care center, retirement community, or animal shelter. Giving renews your connection to your life as well as to those around you. Spend an afternoon roughhousing with toddlers who use you as a jungle gym. Spend an hour in deep conversation with an older person who can't get around very well. Spend time walking and caring for a homeless dog at a pet shelter.

If you feel helpless or hopeless, volunteer at a hospital. Rock and sing an unhappy baby to sleep, deliver flowers and a little strength to a nervous patient, console a family who need a shoulder to cry on. As you care for people who are sick or injured, you'll realize you are far from useless. In fact, your problems may well pale in comparison.

Small gestures mean the most. Meet for coffee with a friend who needs one of your famous heart-to-heart pep talks. Step in at the last minute to help organize the school fund-raiser for the parent who has suffered a family tragedy. Take your neighbor's dog for a walk when he or she is down with the flu. Toss a token in the tollbooth for the person behind you. Buy a hard-working police officer a cup of coffee. Simple acts of caring can turn a bad day around in a flash.

Giving is helping when, where, and how you can. You can donate a few extra ears of corn for the barbecue to raise money for the school band to buy new uniforms or you can bequeath $10,000 to build a new playground. It's all the same. A heartfelt expression of kindness and caring creates compassion for you and motivates others to respond "in kind."

When you keep everything to yourself, including yourself, you believe there is not enough to go around for everyone. Not enough time to share, not enough money to spare, not enough work for two, not enough eligible people for everyone, not enough. There is enough for everyone when we all pitch in.

Don't forget about yourself.

Go for a walk on a crisp fall day. Ask someone to watch your children so you can take yourself to an afternoon movie. Make a date with your wife and rediscover why you fell in love. Delegate a meeting, then go have a quiet cup of coffee where no one can find you. Keep the spark in your soul burning brightly so you can light the way for others.

Giving is receiving when you know that there is always enough to share, and the smile on someone else's face is the best gift of all.

Feel good about taking time to recharge your own batteries so that you can continue to give of yourself. You can't feed your farm animals from an empty barn.

Tend Your Own

CHAPTER 21

I f the cows get loose, the roof blows off the barn during a storm, or the tractor gets stuck in the mud, a dirt farmer can count on her neighbors to be over lickety-split to help put things right. Who can count on you?

You create a sense of community and belonging when you watch out for the people around you.

If your neighbor needs help ripping out an old stump or looking for her lost cat, you help. If someone's home burns down, you go through your closet and find clothes and household goods to donate to the family who lost everything.

These days, families are scattered all over the globe. Mom and Dad may live 1,000 miles away. Big cities are full of strangers whose plight is easy to ignore. But when you become part of a community, you can't ignore people's pain any longer—you take action.

You become part of an extended family and community by helping out *before* being asked. Volunteer to take your friend to the airport. Ask if you can pull in your next-door neighbors' garbage can and mail while they are on vacation. Take a flashlight over to an elderly neighbor during a power outage. Be first in line to fill sandbags during a flood. Help build a new home for a needy family. Work at a homeless shelter serving up hot turkey dinners on Thanksgiving.

Where Dad grew up in Nebraska, helping was fun. During harvest, families would work on one farm until the crop was in, then move to the next farm, until the whole town's fields were cleared of their bounty. Every single person in the community was either helping or being helped.

You can be involved in building your community, near and far. Donate canned goods to the local food bank. Give blankets to victims of an earthquake in Turkey. Help kids learn to read at a nearby elementary school. Host an exchange student from the Ukraine for a year. We are all residents of the same small planet. It is up to us to tend to its growth.

Don't forget to get your kids involved in their community. Help them connect to where they live by volunteering. They could pick up litter at the park or sell cookies to raise money for their baseball team, or plant trees. Help them to learn that giving is as important as receiving.

Tend your own—your own family, neighborhood, community, nation, and even the world—then watch your own crop grow.

Grow or Wither

CHAPTER 22

Hay fields grow constantly. They sprout in spring, shoot up and bloom in summer, are harvested in fall, and gather strength in winter to do it all over again come spring.

It takes a lot to kill hay. Fire might, but only if it gets to the roots. Extended drought could, but one good downpour, and it will pop back. Even too much fertilizer may burn it, but it will still come back, because it is always adapting and growing.

Even as hay lies dormant in winter it's still growing. As your life moves from one season to the next, it's vital that you continue to stretch your boundaries, reach for new experiences, and continue to adapt and grow.

If you've hit a new stage in your life and feel displaced, now is the time to redefine who you are, what you want, where you want to go, and how you're going to get there.

Life is short—don't surrender a single second while you have it. Keep blooming; it's never too late (or early) to push ahead, to learn something new.

Now that you've finished college and have no term papers to write, will you memorize the *TV Guide* and watch hours of Jerry Springer? Or will you sit down in front of a flashing computer screen to write your own compelling literary novel?

When the kids finally move out of the house, will you sit at the kitchen table wondering what to do with your newfound time? Or will you start training for that marathon you've wanted to run since you turned forty?

When you retire, will you sit back in your well-worn Barcalounger™ and call it a life? Or will you take that pottery class you've always talked about but have never taken the time to pursue?

It takes courage to grab and embrace changes that happen in each new phase of your life.

The shifting stages of your life can be scary, but do you want to spend your days living or hiding?

Challenge yourself to experience something new. Go to dinner with a girlfriend and finally try sushi. Learn how to use the Internet so you can stay in touch with your kids via e-mail. Try something that requires a new skill, like yoga or learning another language. Go beyond your comfort zone and travel to Bermuda or Montana by yourself. Continue to push your boundaries and explore this ever-changing world.

When Dad retired, he and Mom moved down to the farm to enjoy a quiet life. Then they realized that, if they were going to live on a farm, they better know something about farming and the soil. So they took a Master Gardener's class. They had a lot of homework and quizzes to pass before they could get certified.

Not only did they both pass with flying colors; they bought a 20' × 70' prefab metal-framed greenhouse to grow their own vegetables and herbs. They reached out to learn something new and, in the process, discovered they could grow—and even sell—herbs on the Oregon coast. They started a new business by taking a class and embracing their new life.

You don't have to wait until you're eighty to feel as if your life is ebbing away. Do you get up, go to work, come home, and go to sleep, just to do the exact same thing tomorrow? Wake up! Don't waste another second sleepwalking through your life. Push your limits. Break out of your routine so you can grow and flourish, and cultivate each new stage of your life.

Step out. Walk through your own hay field of life. Make sure it's healthy and growing regardless of your season.

⬛

Like hay, we are all in a constant state of adapting and growing, whether we know it or not. It actually takes more effort to wither up and blow away than to embrace your evolving life.

Go to the Dance to Dance

CHAPTER 23

To a dirt farmer nothing is as fun as a good old-fashioned barn dance. Horses and plows are cleared from the barn, lights dangle from rafters, and bales of hay become prickly perches. Young and old alike twirl to music rich with fiddles, guitars, and crooning minstrels. Old-timers argue about the weather and swap fish stories.

In the old days, people went to the dance to have fun,
to forget about their worries for a few hours.
They didn't go to sell their crops, find true love,
or swing the deal of the century.

If, however, the farmers did sell their crops, discover ever-lasting love, or strike an outstanding bargain, that was strictly a bonus. It was not the primary reason they joined the hoedown. They went to the dance to dance.

Do things because you want to, not because you believe it might lead to something else. When you participate in activities in which you have a genuine interest, you will never be disappointed with the outcome.

I really needed a date, so I went to a Super Bowl™ party to meet men. I didn't care who was playing; I just thought the gathering would be a perfect place to meet someone who could take me out on the town. After all, men like a cool chick who watches football, right?

As soon as I entered the festively decorated den, I scanned the room for potential targets. I noticed a couple of promising guys hovering by the heaping buffet table and promptly aimed myself in their direction.

I tried to talk with each of them, but to my shock, they were actually watching the game. These guys weren't going to discover what a wonderful woman I was unless I was a beer, a bag of chips, or a touchdown.

Since I honestly had no interest in watching the game and no man at the party was interested in watching me, I left. I was expecting a ton of single men who couldn't wait to get their hands on my . . . phone number. But what I found was a bunch of rowdy guys screaming at the officials. I felt like an idiot. So now I only go to Super Bowl™ parties if I actually want to see the game.

Have you ever signed up for a class in which you had no real interest because it provided a networking opportunity? Have you ever volunteered for a cause not because you valued what it stood for, but because it gave you the opportunity to meet the city's movers and shakers?

Chances are, if you spend your time and money where

you genuinely have passion, concern, or curiosity, you won't lose enthusiasm over time. If you take a class or engage in an activity that you truly enjoy, you'll feel great about being there. And you won't be grumpy even if you don't have a chance to network with the bigwigs or find your perfect mate.

Colleen loves cats and dogs. She volunteers at an animal shelter because she wants to see that all animals find a loving home. The fact that it is a place to meet new and interesting people is a bonus, but it is not the main reason that she volunteers. Colleen is passionate about helping people find the "purrfect" homeless animal and adopt it. If she meets someone special doing what she loves, that's the icing, but not the cake.

If you accept a job you really don't want, but that you believe may lead to a better one, you aren't dancing. You're only waiting until you find a more suitable partner—who may never come.

If you buy a certain car just to show off, you aren't dancing. You're too busy checking yourself out to notice anyone who wants to dance.

If you spend every nickel you earn buying into a lifestyle you can't afford just to impress other people, that's not dancing. That's bragging about dance steps you don't even know.

When you go to the dance to dance, your feet don't get tired, the punch bowl never empties, the music never stops, and the night lasts forever. And don't worry. When you go to the dance to dance, the perfect partner will find you.

Under Overalls

CHAPTER 24

Overalls are a dirt farmer's uniform. They have loops to hold tools, a special slot to keep your pencil handy, and the bib is a great place to keep your hands warm. They may not be fancy, but they're just what you need when you're mucking out the barn.

Everyone wears a uniform of some kind. Some people wear $2,000 suits to their office; others wear swim trunks to their job at the beach. Some women are so busy chasing kids they can't remember what they have on; others spend hours choosing just the right outfit to sign a big contract.

Clean or dirty, expensive or cheap, uniforms only cover what is underneath; they're not who we are. Under our overalls, we're all the same.

It is important to respect someone's expertise, knowledge, ability, or position, but you don't have to feel intimidated by that person. Meet these gifted, skilled, or educated people on equal ground. Because, the truth is, regardless of their overalls, you're both the same under them.

A dirt farmer knows who he is (or at least who he wants to be). He works hard, he's humble, he doesn't take his blessings for granted, and he knows his worth. He may toil in muddy fields, fix equipment, and round up livestock, but he can walk into a meeting with a banker, lawyer, or engineer and feel as secure as if he were riding atop his tractor.

Dad had a keen interest in my academic progress so he scheduled a meeting with my high-school principal. He walked into the principal's office and was offered a seat in a student's smaller chair sitting in front of the principal's sinister wooden desk. Refusing to be intimidated by the surroundings, the principal, or that silly chair, he simply sat on the corner of the principal's desk. Smiling, he extended his hand and said, "Hi. How are you doing, Stan?" The principal was suddenly and uncharacteristically scared to death—which he confessed to my dad years later. It is hard to feel intimidated, nervous, or out of place when you picture people wearing overalls, a straw hat perched on their head, and a piece of hay hanging out of the corner of their mouth.

Admire someone for the success she enjoys in her career, but don't feel less worthy for choosing to do something that doesn't appear to be as glamorous. Not everyone can be the CEO of a Fortune 500 company or a movie star. We need people to raise our food, repair our plumbing, and fix our cars.

Be respectful to people who hold public office or a position of authority. But remember that you are an essential part of the process that keeps them in their powerful positions. You have every right to speak up and state your opinion.

Look to your boss for advice and guidance, but don't demean yourself to obtain a promotion. Keep your head down, work hard, and get that raise on your own merits.

Wear your overalls with pride. It makes no difference if they are covered with grease, mud, perfume, or pinstripes, because underneath we are all equal.

Spritz Your Petals or You'll Go to Seed

CHAPTER 25

I n the dirt farmer's garden, there are shrubs that require little care to flourish and bloom, while others demand daily attention to produce even a single flower. To encourage new buds to develop it's important to prune wilted petals, loosen dirt around the plant's footing, and spritz the plant with water. If you don't take a few minutes to tend the plant, it will dwindle while in bloom, then go to seed.

Just like a beautiful shrub, you will go to seed
if you don't take time, a few minutes, an evening,
or even a weekend, to spritz your own petals.

When Mom and Dad moved permanently out of the big city to a tranquil farm life, Dad figured he could relax and would never wear a suit and tie again. Everyone knows farmers wear jeans and boots, right? Mom agreed and tossed out her six-inch heels in favor of garden clogs.

Well, after about three years of nothing but muddy boots, clogs, tattered jeans, and sweat-stained baseball hats, Mom and Dad had gone to seed. Dad was sporting a scruffy beard, and Mom had stopped coloring her hair. Then one day, as they were planning a trip to San Francisco, they caught sight of their reflections in the mirror. They hardly recognized themselves.

It was time to replant. They realized that they had stopped caring about their appearance and it was time for action. They got out of their grubby, hardworking farm clothes, spritzed their petals, and went out on the town.

They signed up for a dance class where they could wear whatever they wanted, including jeans and tennis shoes. But it helped them to wear shoes in which they could tango. That meant Mom had to dig out her beautiful high heels and Dad his polished wing tips. From then on, they wore nice outfits to match their fancy dancing shoes.

Now they dance two to three times a week and go to lavish galas five times a year. Although they still wear boots, clogs, and jeans to work the farm, Dad is now the proud owner of his own tuxedo, and Mom has the opportunity to wear every dazzling shoe in her closet. They figured out how to be farmers and spritz their petals.

*You don't have to live in the country
to let yourself go to seed.*

Inundated with projects at the office, you may put off going to the gym for a badly needed physical and mental workout. You can't find a spare second, between keeping your home organized and carting the kids around, to schedule an appointment for a haircut. Spritzing your petals doesn't have to cost anything. You could

- Trade manicures and pedicures with a girlfriend
- Swap massages with your honey
- Shave off your facial hair and expose your handsome face
- Take a nice long walk
- Indulge in a bubble bath until the water becomes cold, and then fill up the tub again
- Turn off the phone, computer, and TV, and enjoy the quiet
- Take a dream-filled nap

Dress up, take yourself out, and show off your sparkling petals. People will be glad to see the real you. And so will you!

The Price of Dreams

CHAPTER 26

A dirt farmer knows the price she pays for living the life she wants. She willingly trades a six-figure salary for sunshine and freedom, and a full social calendar for quiet evenings by a blazing fire.

———

To the dirt farmer the cost of savoring her dreams is worth every penny. What are you willing to sacrifice, endure, or pay to get the life you want?

For a couple of years, I had a traveling sales job that paid me a sizable salary, with tremendous perks and benefits. I truly enjoyed the weekly travel, the new cities I got to see, and my work. It was fun, exciting, and extremely fulfilling. Until I got a new boss.

I liked Bob. He had a good sense of humor, worked hard, and seemed to support his staff. Besides, I never saw him. I only spoke with him on the phone once a week. It never occurred to me that my working life could change. But change it did, and dramatically.

Every time I spoke with him, he made me feel like I was

the worst salesperson in the world. The job was physically and emotionally demanding—travelling five days a week always is—but I never questioned the toll on my body and mind until Bob told me I wasn't doing enough. Nothing I did was ever good enough, no contract large enough, my sixty-hour workweek was not long enough, and a personal life was out of the question.

After our conversations each Monday, I cried until I couldn't breathe. I began to hate the life and job I once loved.

What were my dreams worth? Was this what I wanted to endure for the rest of my life? Should I quit even though I didn't have another job? What was I willing to sacrifice to achieve my dreams?

I quit. My dream life didn't include being verbally abused, feeling worthless, and working beyond all reason, while allowing myself no real life at all. I valued my dreams, and I wasn't about to sell them to someone who didn't appreciate or care about me.

Is your job killing your soul? Are you putting up with poor treatment because you think it will get you closer to your dream?

⟶

*Nothing good comes easy. You have to work hard
for the life you want.*

⟵

It requires determination, dedication, and an iron will to move beyond the storms and into the rainbow. But you never have to sell yourself short in the process.

Angela is an actor. She works hard every day to become better at her craft by taking classes, rehearsing monologues, getting prepared for auditions, and learning the business of being an actor.

She decided long ago that she would not sell herself short for a possible opportunity. She was offered a number of roles with nudity, which she turned down. A challenging role was presented to her if she would have sex with the producer. She said, "no thank you," and passed. It might have made her famous, but the price was her self-respect, and she wasn't willing to pay it.

Angela might not be a celebrated actor yet, but she is working with dignity and her dreams are still intact. She knows what price she is willing to pay for her dreams to come true. She also knows what she is willing to give up to protect her spirit.

Do you have the life you always dreamed of? Are you pursuing the life you want or waiting until the time is right to begin the journey?

Don't sell yourself short. Your dreams take time, effort, and determination to come true. Make sure you know the price of your dreams before the check is set on the table.

*You Won't Be Remembered for Your
Fleet of Tractors*

CHAPTER 27

Today a tractor is an indispensable piece of farm equipment to the dirt farmer. Instead of taking days, the tractor plows fields in hours. It cuts harvest to market time in half and reduces the backbreaking labor that used to be required to farm with horses.

Tractors might be great, but you only need one to get the job done on a small farm.

If you spend your time focused on obtaining a bigger, faster, and more deluxe tractor, or several of them, you lose sight of why you got the tractor to begin with—to simplify your life. A fulfilling life comes from the knowledge that we are enough, without the decorations, accessories, or possessions that we display.

Dana and Tom had promising careers working at the same high-tech company. They fell in love and got married. When they began their professional life, they put in long hours, struggled to make ends meet, and enjoyed every second of it.

As their workload expanded, so did their salaries. They no longer worried about every penny at the grocery store; they could afford to buy a new car, and planned to buy a house.

After a couple more years of working their butts off, their salaries and stock options were enormous. They bought their first home—their dream home—with four bedrooms and a water view, two new cars, had a beautiful baby boy, and had to hire a nanny because they were never home.

They had everything. Gorgeous furniture to fill up their elegant home, trendy cars to buzz around in, and the latest fashions to impress their colleagues. They also had no time to enjoy the spoils of all their efforts because they had to pay for their lavish lifestyle.

Dana would have loved to stay home with her growing son, but they couldn't afford to be without her salary. They maxed out their credit cards to buy all their designer furniture; their car and house payments were overwhelming. They couldn't even spare the money for a weekend vacation.

On the outside Dana and Tom had all the trappings of the perfect life. But inside neither of them was happy. Not in the least. They spent all their time working, buying, and gathering beautiful, expensive, trendy, top-of-the-line things, which turned out to be just a bunch of stuff.

*When your tractor becomes more important than
your family, your friends, or your self-respect,
it's time to sell it.*

When I was little, I lived across the street from an older Japanese lady who didn't speak English very well. For years, I would spend hours with Mrs. Iwashda as she gardened in her backyard. For two people of such different backgrounds and ages, we had a very loving relationship.

When she died, my heart was broken. I remember sitting in my bedroom window, looking at her house, longing for her to walk out her door and gesture for me to come over for cookies. For weeks after she died, I would wander over to her house, forgetting she was gone. Then I would remember. And it would hurt all over again.

When her son cleared out her house, he brought over two things she wanted me to have. One was a beautiful black lacquered jewelry box painted with scenes of Japan on all sides. A silver lock protected precious mementos. The key lay in one of the bottom drawers with a silk string attached to one of the pulls so it wouldn't get lost.

The second gift was from her prized jewelry collection. It was a small goldfish carved out of yellow and white jade.

The craftsmanship was so superb that the fish appeared to be swimming from the necklace on which it hung.

I cherish these items more than anything else, and I think of my beautiful Japanese friend every day. But I would miss her kind, loving spirit even if I didn't have those thoughtful gifts to remind me of her.

When you die, no one is going to remember you for your fleet of tractors. Your family, neighbors, and colleagues will only recall the time they spent with the person who drove the tractors.

Ego Cutting Off the Air to Your Brain?

CHAPTER 28

*A dirt farmer is humble because she knows
that nothing is constant except change.*

B ad luck can turn into good fortune with the ring of
the telephone; a profitable crop can become a barren
field with a passing hailstorm; a person who thinks
he is invincible can become crippled when ego cuts off the
air to his brain.

Your ego is your ally when you are faced with difficult,
uncomfortable, or challenging situations because it's the
part of you that defends and protects your individuality. But
it has the potential to severely damage every area of your
life when it is allowed to distort and consume who you are.

Your ego gains a foothold when you become disconnected from what's really important in your life. If you're a
doctor who saves lives during the day, yet you come home
feeling too important to fix a clogged toilet, your ego has
taken control, and you have lost touch.

Your ego grabs control when it leads you to believe that
you will never be knocked off that pedestal you've put yourself on. People might tell you how brilliant you are at your

job. Instead of accepting praise with humility and taking it with a grain of salt, you let your ego take over. You believe every word and actually see yourself that way. Your ego goes on to convince you that you can't be replaced.

Guess what? You can always be replaced. No matter what your position: president, plumber, parent, or prosecutor.

Kelly worked his fingers to the bone seven days a week for five years to get his toy manufacturing business off the ground. All his dedication and sacrifice finally paid off when one of his toys hit the big time. The demand was so overwhelming, he couldn't keep the toy in stock. He began to take individual orders for $100,000 instead of $100. Suddenly he was making mountains of money, taking phone calls from corporate presidents, and approaching the pinnacle of the toy industry.

After two years of unbridled success, it all fell apart. Kelly's ego had taken control of his business. He began to snap at loyal employees, took two-hour lunches to indulge himself, didn't bother to return phone calls, and was rude to some of his long-time customers. Unfortunately, no one criticized his behavior during his ego trip. Customers felt he was giving them something special. Employees were afraid he might fire them. No one would pop his ego bubble.

However, at the next international trade show, a brand-new toy came out, becoming the next sensation. Surprise—the season had changed.

Everyone forgot about Kelly's bauble. He didn't believe it could happen to him because his product had been on fire for so long. He couldn't imagine anyone could extinguish his long run.

Now, without the assistance of those loyal customers and employees who had helped build his initial empire—they left—Kelly was back working seven days a week with no lunch break just to keep his business afloat.

Your ego is helpful when it's kept in check. It can spur you on to submit your resumé one more time after so many rejections because you know you are talented and qualified. It can make you pack your bags and leave a relationship that isn't healthy because you know you are worthy of something better.

Use your ego to help you succeed. Just don't let it devour you once you have achieved your goal.

Like a dirt farmer, remain humble in the face of your hard-won success.

Be grateful for your bounty. Your fortunes could change at any moment, and you still have to go home and plow the field.

You Don't Get What You Don't Ask For

CHAPTER 29

When the tractor gets stuck in the mud during a spring squall, a dirt farmer can't leave his equipment to the mercy of the elements. No matter what time of day it is, a dirt farmer can call a friend to bring his truck to help pull him out.

A dirt farmer always asks for what he needs and wants. By taking the chance of asking, he increases the possibility of actually getting it.

Down on the farm every penny you save makes a big difference. A 2 percent discount on grain to feed the cattle might not sound like much, but it adds up over the years. Still, you must ask for it, to get it. And as the growing season comes to an end, it's crucial to ask for extra help to bring in the harvest.

During my last quarter in college I finally got around to taking an art class. Since I couldn't draw to save my life, pottery was my only option.

I learned how to knead clay to the proper consistency, to use sponges to get a smooth finish, and to coat my pieces with colorful glaze to get just the right sheen.

To show us how to properly glaze our pots, my professor pulled out his current project. His work took my breath away. The vase he casually placed on the workbench was a blank canvas of white porcelain. The full-bodied vessel was gently stretched to make the mouth into the shape of an almond. It was sturdy enough to hold dozens of roses, but appeared to be fragile, as if it would break with a harsh word.

My professor pulled a straw from his plaid shirt pocket, jabbed it into an old soup can full of mysterious liquid and bent down, taking a quick pull. He lifted it up and blew the contents through the straw. A splash of color exploded on the white vase, leaving a trail of blue tears dripping beneath it. He plunged the straw into another soup can.

He repeated this process, blowing six or seven colors as he gently turned the vase clockwise. He held my rapt attention while he explained that the colors intensify when fired in the kiln. As he finished his demonstration, the vase looked like kids had splattered it with a squirt gun full of color. It was beautiful and it wasn't even fired yet. I was so impressed, I asked him if I could have it.

I couldn't believe my own gall, but honestly, I didn't think he would take me seriously. To my amazement, he cocked his head to one side, smiled, and said, "Sure." He left me standing with my mouth open and the other students were looking at me with total surprise and, no doubt, a twinge of jealousy.

A couple of classes went by, and I forgot about my brash request for the vase, until he stood in front of me with it in hand, asking if I still wanted it. Yes. Yes, please.

He casually handed me his magnificent objet d'art. I cradled the vase gently. I couldn't believe my good luck, but then again, I did ask for it.

I still have that vase, and every time I look at it, it reminds me to ask for what I want.

⸺

Ask for what you want, even if you don't get it.
You will be no worse off for your effort,
and it might just pay off in spades.

⸺

Some dear friends were moving, so we got together for a farewell dinner. We ended up at a seafood restaurant, which was teeming with customers.

We waited in the bar for forty-five minutes before we were seated. Our polite waiter brought water, then disappeared. By the time he showed up again to take our order we were starving, and becoming agitated. We waited patiently for our food to arrive, but nearly an hour passed after we ordered.

I found the manager and asked nicely if there was a backup in the kitchen. I didn't scream or yell, although my stomach was ready to take no prisoners. I told him how long we had been waiting. He said he would take care of the problem immediately.

True to his word, he came to our table and gave us the bad news. They had lost our order. He said they were making it right now, and he graciously offered us free dessert.

By the time our food finally arrived a half hour later, we weren't hungry. We looked at our meals with mild disgust and pushed the plates of otherwise delicious food away. When the waiter showed up to ask how our "late" meals were, we frowned and said, "We're not hungry anymore."

At this point, we asked for what we wanted. Free meals. The manager was actually happy to accommodate us, and wished us happy trails.

Ask for what you want. Be brave.

Muster up your courage and ask your boss for the raise you deserve. In fact, ask for a larger one—you have nothing to lose.

Calm your nerves if you get your car back from the mechanic and it still makes those funny clicks when you hit the gas. Drive back to the garage and ask them to fix it. It doesn't make any difference if the car has to go back ten times.

When you ask for what you want, you have the power to make it happen. People won't give you anything until you ask.

Don't be disappointed if you don't get it. Just because you didn't get what you asked for today, doesn't mean you won't tomorrow. Keep asking. Your chances of success increase greatly every time you ask.

You can ask for the life you want, too. Ask for anything, but remember to be specific. Small details make a huge difference with your outcome.

You can ask for

- A partner who . . .
- A job that is . . .
- A income of . . .
- A house that has . . .
- A car that . . .
- A body that . . .
- A spiritual life containing . . .

Have courage. Ask for what you want. Nothing is too outlandish or too insignificant to request.

On the farm, every little push puts you closer to your goal, the life you want. The life you ask for.

No Sacred Cows

CHAPTER 30

In India, some people believe that cows are sacred beings. They will not use them for food, even if the village is starving. They honor cows and create shrines for them; under no circumstances will their cows be harmed. These are sacred cows.

On dirt farms, however, most cows are raised for milk or food. Next to raising crops, milk cows and beef cattle are a basic livelihood.

Dirt farmers care for their livestock with kindness and respect. But dirt farmers have no sacred cows. They can't afford to.

Harboring no sacred cows in your family means that everything is open for discussion.

Nothing is off-limits. Any topic, idea, philosophy, or belief is welcomed at the dinner table.

One chilly fall evening, my family and some visiting friends sat in the front room, lights off, watching the fire pop and crackle. Four adults and four teenagers sat snugly curled up in chairs, enjoying deep conversation. This was something I had done many times with my folks, so I took it for granted that everyone's family did it.

In the dark, cozy room, we were comfortable expressing our opinions in muted tones as the discussion moved seamlessly from one topic to another. We talked about everything— school, peer pressure, drugs, politics, sex, the environment, money. We encouraged one another to participate. We asked questions.

The blazing fire burned down to glowing embers. None of us wanted to go to bed. We shared our thoughts, gave different perspectives, solved problems, and discussed the so-called generation gap.

Dad told me later that our friends had never heard their kids talk like that before. For the first time, they had a better understanding of their children because their children felt free to talk in the darkness, and they actually listened to them. They discovered their kids knew much more about life than they had given them credit for. It opened their eyes and made room for further discussions.

～

*When families, couples, or even companies shelter
sacred cows, it can destroy them.*

～

Some parents aren't comfortable talking about sex with their kids. They can barely explain the basic birds and bees theory, let alone the complexities of having sex too early, sexually transmitted diseases, and how to protect yourself from getting someone pregnant, or becoming pregnant. Guaranteed—kids will find another source of information on any topic if parents are not willing to talk about it.

Having no sacred cows in a relationship is the basis for discovering and working through problems. Some couples are uneasy discussing money, which is one of the primary reasons cited for the implosion of relationships. One partner wants to save for a rainy day, while the other makes immediate plans to buy a boat. The problem is not that they have different financial goals. The problem is that they're not sharing their goals with one another. If you aren't willing to discuss every issue in a relationship, your failure to communicate will sink it.

Some companies are afraid to be honest with their employees when the company is in trouble. But employees are the best source of information to explain why and how the company is failing. When you don't have any sacred cows and everyone is free to talk about problems and share ideas for solutions, anyone from the janitor to the CEO could be the one to save the day, not to mention everyone's job.

Granted, it can be very difficult to talk about things that make you uncomfortable. But that's exactly the moment you need to talk about them. The hardest sentence is the first one. So speak from your heart and let the conversation begin.

Before you get married, be sure to seek out your own sacred cows and expose them. If you want kids, make sure your partner does too, before you say, "I do."

During a job interview, ask tough questions. Ask about unspoken company policies. Do they expect you to work late and every weekend, leaving you no time to spend with your family? Make sure all your questions are answered and that everything is out in the open before you decide to take the job.

When you keep your thoughts locked up, they don't go away. They only grow stronger. Secrets fester.

Sometimes the help of a professional may be needed to get the discussion rolling. Contact a counseling group, therapist, or your religious advisor if you want extra support. Your local crisis hot line, which you can find in your telephone book, has a complete list of groups, organizations, and contacts.

I enjoy talking with my parents about anything. Although we don't always agree, we do have rousing discussions. Mom has a magnet on the refrigerator that says, "You can agree with me, or you can be wrong." It is the running joke of the family.

Mom and Dad have spirited opinions about everything, especially when it comes to me and my life. Politics: mine are wrong. Money: I should be saving more for retirement. Relationships: when am I going to find a nice boy and settle down?

Through it all, I never worry that my folks will stop loving me if I challenge their ideas. We talk, argue, discuss, and end with a hug and kiss.

Having no sacred cows requires you to respect other people's ideas, opinions, and thoughts. Be sure to keep an open mind, just in case they might have a valid point.

Spend time dismantling the shrines to your sacred cows and let the light flood into the dark places of fear. Enjoy the debate as you watch the ideas flow.

Your Word

CHAPTER 31

When a dirt farmer needs help repairing a broken fence post or chasing down a lost calf and his neighbor says she'll be there, he can count on her, come hell or high water.

When you stand behind what you say, no one doubts you or your sincerity. You are not only honest with others, but you are honest with yourself.

Dix was a giant of a man. He stood six feet seven inches in his bare feet and weighed over 350 pounds. He was one of the gentlest men I have ever known. He was called upon often to help his small Oregon coast community because of his size and strength, but he was also unbelievably smart.

If Dix said he would be there to help, people could count on him like the tide ebbing and flowing. If, however, he didn't specifically state that he would be there, no one expected him.

Dix was always as good as his word. He never disappointed anyone, including himself.

When you stand behind your word, you're trustworthy.

If someone asks you to work the corn on the cob stand at the annual country fair and you don't have time, say so. Say no. Don't say yes, and then not show up, leaving everyone scrambling to find your replacement.

Ed was a nice guy with good intentions who always said yes to everything. But most of the time he didn't show up. He said yes to so many people that he lost track of his commitments. When the time arrived for Ed to show up, he became too embarrassed to call and cancel, so he just flaked out.

No one will stop being your friend if you say no. You will lose friends, however, if you constantly disappoint people who rely on you, who want to trust you. Ed lost friends.

Everyone understands that there are only so many hours in the day, and that everyone has obligations. But it's a deal breaker when you are left in the lurch after someone you counted on doesn't come through.

If you are a parent, do you keep your word to yourself about caring for your children? Do you keep your word to them?

If you own a business, do you keep deadlines you set for yourself? Do you follow through with your employees when you say you will?

Are you as good as your word? Stand behind your commitments. Be faithful to your obligations. Only then will you have the trust of the world behind you.

Dirt farmers can't afford not to trust their own word. The survival of the farm and their families depends on them. Chickens need to be fed, cows need to be milked, the equipment needs upkeep, and the fields need attention. These chores can't wait.

You Can't Catch Water with a Fist

Dirt farmers used to hand-pump their water. They had no convenient spigots that easily turned on and off. As the water gushed from the worn iron spout, they cupped their hands to catch as much as they could hold for a deep drink or to splash on their dirty face.

They cupped their hands because it's impossible to catch water with a fist. The same is true for grasping innovative ideas, groundbreaking information, and original inventions. You can't understand and use them if your mind is closed like a fist.

Opening your mind is essential to catching new thoughts that you can explore and use, just as your cupped hands catch running water.

Farming isn't an exact science. What works miracles in one region may cause great harm in another. That's why it's crucial to share new ideas and information. With expanding technology shrinking the world, local ideas quickly become global. Concepts that a farmer might have thought absurd before, such as rotation grazing and pasture management, now must be seriously considered. But valuable information won't help you if you are closed off to receiving it.

You don't have to embrace unfamiliar opinions like a long-lost cousin, but it's good practice not to summarily dismiss them out of hand as fancy or folly.

Unlike Bedstefar, my maternal grandfather didn't like change. He was neither inspired nor excited by inventions that would actually make his life easier. As the world progressed around him, he fought progress with every breath and refused to take advantage of modern technology.

The rustic vacation cabin on Lake Thomas had been in his family for generations. For decades it had only a wood cookstove, candles, and lanterns. It took him years to hook up electricity. He slammed his fist down when it came to putting in a telephone. He complained that there had never been a telephone at the cabin, there was no reason for one, and who the hell was going to call him anyway?

One year, during his annual fall hunting trip, when he stayed at the cabin, my grandmother died. He couldn't be reached because there was no phone at the lake house. A county sheriff was dispatched to find him, break the news, then drive him back to town.

We can only wonder what he must have been feeling

when he had a telephone installed a week after my grandmother's funeral. That was his last trip to the cabin.

Are you stuck in one mode of thinking? Do you still believe that life was better in the fifties, sixties, or seventies? Are you hanging on to the "good old days," without even checking out the possibility of a "good new day"?

New doesn't always mean "improved" on the farm. Sometimes the old ways are the best. But you'll never know until you check new ideas for sturdiness and decide if they fit into your life. Then, and only then, will you be drinking your fill from cupped hands.

~~~

It's time to cup those hands and allow new ideas
to gush into your life. Indulge yourself. Think up new
ideas of your own. It makes no difference if other people
think your inventions are silly. They are all yours.
People thought airplanes were crazy too.
Let those new ideas flow.

Be True to Yourself

CHAPTER 33

A cow is a cow. It can't pretend to be a chicken, horse, or goat. The cow doesn't spend any time thinking about how to be a cow. It simply lives the truth of being one.

Unlike people, cows don't ask friends if their swollen udder makes them look fat or if their stripes and spots are out of fashion. A cow is simply a cow.

Dogs don't care if you're a doctor or a garbage collector as long as you love them, care for them, and treat them with kindness. Their truth is love, and nothing less.

What is your truth? Are you happy in your career or would you rather be a circus clown? Is your relationship worth working on every day or would you rather live alone with fifteen cats? What is your truth?

Mom and Dad always asked us what we wanted to do when we grew up. I changed my mind every week. One week I wanted to be a French-speaking marine biologist, the next a child protection attorney, and the next a superstar. My brother Phil, on the other hand, always knew what he wanted to be.

While we were sitting around the dinner table, Phil, who was in fourth grade at the time, announced that he was going to be a dentist. That was that. His truth pushed him forward every day.

Phil played college baseball. He was a remarkably gifted pitcher who practiced for hours daily with the team, while taking a heavy load of grueling science classes. During one practice, he caught a forceful line drive, injuring his right-hand fingers. Fortunately, he is left-handed. But it finally occurred to him that if he wanted to be a dentist, healthy fingers and hands would be crucial to his practice. He quit baseball the next day.

When you live your truth, you won't spend time thinking how you are going to do it. You just do it.

From the time Molly was twelve, the only thing she ever wanted to be was a wife and mother. After high school she went on to college and received her bachelor's degree in communications, married her college sweetheart, and began to plan a large family.

She had three kids in four years and couldn't be happier. She runs the house, ferries the children from one activity to another, and manages the family finances, while her husband works to support the family.

Molly's college friends give her nothing but grief

because she doesn't use her education to work outside the home. But she is very clear about what her truth is. She is a wife and a mother, and she loves it.

When she is finished being CEO of her family, and her children are grown and gone, she can go on to pursue managing any other enterprise she wishes. Can you say that about your life?

If you are wondering what your truth is, one way to discover it is to remember what thing you did that made you happy as a child.

- Did you love bugs?
- Did you love to draw?
- Did you love to talk with your friends for hours?
- Did you love to crack jokes and make people laugh?
- Did you love to write?
- Did you love math?
- Did you love to play in the dirt?

Be true to yourself about who you are, what you want, and how you want to live. Are you living the life someone else wants for you, or are you living the life that makes you happy?

Remember, a cow is a cow because it doesn't pretend to be anything or anyone else.

Don't Count on Rain

CHAPTER 34

Through the years, dirt farmers have had to rely on rain to water their fields. They hoped for a deep, soaking shower to quench their dry crops during the summer. But they feared a deluge, because an unrelenting downpour would wash them away.

They wanted to count on rain, but the unfortunate truth is that drought strikes in cycles, some of them lasting for years. Dirt farmers were forced to find a crop-watering remedy or lose their farms—their way of life.

Here are dirt farmer wisdom problem-solving steps:

1. Define the real problem.
2. Brainstorm.
3. Make a plan of action.
4. Work your plan.

It's easy to complain about the obstacles you face. What makes dirt farmers so powerful is that they don't get mired in rehashing the problem. They define it in a way that helps them actively pursue a solution.

When it comes to finding water for the fields, this is how dirt farmers solve the problem:

Step one: Clearly define the *real* problem.

Outsiders saw the problem as dirt farmers not being able to count on rain. While dirt farmers, realizing that creating rain is completely out of their control, saw the real issue as their crops needing water.

When you define a problem in such a way that you make yourself a victim with no power to tackle the situation, you will always lose the farm.

But the dirt farmer puts herself in the empowered position of explaining the problem in a way that provides a workable solution. In some cases, the problem's definition may well include the answer you're looking for.

Step two: Brainstorming.

No idea is too complex or too simple, too crazy, or too run-of-the-mill. When you brainstorm don't forget to include the most outlandish or simple ideas.

The brainstorming challenge for dirt farmers was how to get water to their fields. They could drill for water, plow canals, hire a Native American to perform a rain dance, or change the type of crops they grew.

My family always seemed to produce torrential downpours when we put up a tent for a weekend of camping. I wouldn't recommend this as a solution to drought, but it might be worth a try.

What dirt farmers actually settled on was the oldest idea: irrigation.

Step three: Create a plan of action.

Farmers had to do hours of research to make irrigation a reality. It was a daunting task. In some areas there were no lakes, streams, or rivers. Or a watershed might belong to someone who wasn't keen on sharing it. The available water might also be polluted. Dirt farmers had to construct pipelines, install hoses and sprinkler heads, and find the money to pay for their irrigation inventions. All this had to be finished in a crop-saving time line. Their game plan was crucial.

Step four: Work the plan.

Once they decided on a plan, they had to work it day in, day out; month in, month out; year in, year out, until they got the life-saving water to their crops. Some dug slender canals down the middle of their fields. Some scooped out deep ponds and laid irrigation pipe, using generators to pull the water into their fields. Some even laid out enormous water barrels to catch the rain, then pumped it to their crops. Their reward for their hard work and determination to find a solution was crops that could withstand cyclical droughts, so they could save their land and maintain their way of life.

If you need a job, don't count on rain. Become your own rainmaker. Define the real problem, brainstorm, make a plan, then work it.

The problem isn't that you don't have a job; you know that. The real issue is that you need to find one.

Brainstorm. What do you want to do? What does your perfect job look like? How much money do you want to earn? Do you want a job in a different industry than the one you have worked in for the last twenty years? Do you want to start your own business? Do you want to go back to school and train for a completely different career? Think about what you want to do, and be honest with yourself. Anything is possible.

Make a plan. Is your resumé updated? Do you need more education? Where can you get the training to get your next position? Where can you network? Is there an internship you can apply for? Come up with a workable plan. Write it out. If you need help, there are career counselors who can help you discover what you want and how to get it.

Finally, work your plan. Distribute your resumé. Network. Call and make appointments with prospective employers. Contact people who are in the same industry to gain insight and allies. Keep working your plan until it becomes a success.

There is a solution to every problem. It might take years

to achieve, but as long as you keep working your plan, modifying it along the way, you will get your problem solved.

Kara is a poet. Her words can move you from pain to understanding, from tears to joy. She wanted to make a living as a poet, so she decided to become her own rainmaker.

First she defined her "problem" the dirt farmer way—realistically. It wasn't that she couldn't make money being a poet; it was that she had to find a way for her passion to produce an income.

She brainstormed, made a plan, and worked it daily. Today, she is no longer just a simple country poet; she publishes an online poetry journal, produces books, and teaches classes on the value of the written word. Her passion pays her bills and gives her the life she always imagined.

Don't lose time getting stuck in your problems. Empower yourself. Define your challenges in a way that empowers you to solve them.

⟶

Work your plan and watch as you become
your own rainmaker.

Corn Grows in Alaska

Alaska, one of the last great frontiers. Winter is dark, bitter, cold, and long, and summer all too short. But Alaskans make the most of it by using what is available. During the summer in northern Alaska, the sun doesn't set for eighty-four days. That's 2016 hours of straight sunshine.

They grow cabbages that weigh eighty-five pounds, they raise beets in half the time of a continental U.S. farmer, and corn can grow sky-high in a matter of weeks.

For corn to grow in Alaska, it took one person to believe it could be done, and then to plant a seed.

If people can grow corn in the harsh, unforgiving terrain of Alaska, then anything is possible, if you believe it is. It takes courage to believe in what other people tell you is impossible.

When Heather changed companies, she negotiated a $25,000-a-year raise in salary to begin her new job. She had the education and background to command the six-figure income and the experience that made her worth every penny.

Her friend Monica was astounded. She didn't have any idea that a person could get that much of a salary increase simply by changing jobs. She never thought she could do it, so she assumed that it was simply impossible.

If you believe that something is impossible, it will be. It will be very difficult to achieve your goals if you don't believe in them, heart and soul.

Vonnie is a talented actor. She moved from Iowa to Hollywood to pursue her dream of acting on the big screen. She signed up for advanced classes, performed in actor showcases, found a skilled agent, and was called for dozens of auditions.

She didn't lack the talent or drive to succeed in a competitive industry. She lacked a belief in herself.

She listened to people who told her how cutthroat the business could be and how so few actually succeed. She took to heart every bit of negative feedback she received during rehearsals, auditions, and meetings. She cried herself to sleep when people told her they loved her work but she didn't have the right look for the part. Instead of taking all those bits and bites of "impossible" and turning them into motivation to continue fighting for her dream, she gave up and headed back to Iowa.

There once was a little girl named Oprah. She was told that she was too fat, too black, too outspoken, and would never succeed in a television career. But she had a rock solid belief in herself and what she wanted to accomplish in her life. She pursued her dreams with dogged persistence and didn't let anyone shake her from her goals.

Don't believe people when they tell you "it" can't be done. If corn grown in Alaska can feed a hungry mob on the Fourth of July, you can do anything you set your mind to.

The world is changing at the speed of light. Technology is breaking barriers that were once deemed science fiction. None of these remarkable inventions could have turned into reality if the inventors had listened to the people who didn't believe in them or what they were doing.

Plant corn wherever you live. Nourish the stalks with kind words, fertilize the roots with determination, and spritz the buds with gratitude. Your dreams can come true when you know corn grows sky-high in Alaska.

Think Simple

The techno-farmer down the lane gets up before dawn, opens his prefabricated metal greenhouse doors, enters the expansive complex, checks the temperature control panel and humidifier, resets the light filters, adjusts the water purifier, then pushes the button that turns on the generator that operates all the sprinkling, fertilizing, and lighting systems. The dirt farmer waters her plants.

When faced with a decision, a problem, a dilemma, or a teenager, think simple.

Thinking simple doesn't necessarily mean easy;
it means looking for the clearest, most concise,
uncomplicated, and effective choice available.

Marie loved Peter. She was ready to get married, settle down, have kids and cats, and get down to the business of growing old together.

They danced in circles for months, heatedly discussing commitment, marriage, and their future. Marie gave Peter ultimatums. She threatened to leave him if he wouldn't set a wedding date. She even tried to bribe Peter with a honeymoon in Tahiti. Nothing worked. She needed to think simple.

Marie could go on in a relationship that might or might not have a future, or she could cut her ties and move on with her life.

She broke up with Peter. Her choice may have been simple, but it was far from easy.

Simple answers are easy to dismiss when you are searching frantically for solutions. The simple idea is the one you tend to reject at first because it seems too basic to actually work. But a simple solution always warrants a second, even a third, look.

If you don't want your kids to smoke, you could take them to an antismoking clinic. You could show them pictures of black lungs full of cancer. You could visit patients who have emphysema, who can barely breathe with an oxygen mask and have tubes up their nose. Or you can think simple. Take the cigarette out of your own mouth and never smoke again.

Say you are up to your eyebrows in debt. You could cut up your credit cards. Get financial advice. Look into a consolidation loan. Take a second job. File for bankruptcy. Or you can think simple. Quit spending money.

If you want your company to reduce expenses you could

have company-wide seminars on how to reduce costs. Pass out books on expense management. Hire a consulting firm to do a research study. Or you could think simple. As company president, cut your own expenses. Show your staff how it's done and be a great role model. Simple. But not easy.

You must walk your talk when you think and preach simple. If your car is "nickel and diming" you to death, you could spend $100 a week on small repairs, quit your job and go to work for a mechanic, park your car on a busy street and hope it gets hit for the insurance, buy a new car you can't afford, marry a mechanic, or you could think simple. Take the bus until you save up for a car that is dependable.

Some people thrive on making situations far more complicated than they have to be. Think of it this way: the absolute opposite of thinking simple is government.

When your cows break through the pasture fence, do you call a committee meeting, initiate an environmental impact study, and call in the National Guard?
Or do you simply catch your cows and mend the fence?

Think simple. Stay on track. Don't allow yourself to be led in another direction that has nothing to do with the issue at hand, no matter what anyone else says. Define the problem the dirt farmer way, in clear, concise terms, and push for an uncomplicated, immediate plan of action.

Don't complicate your life by looking for messy solutions. Think simple. You don't have to have a greenhouse full of expensive equipment to water your plants.